DROP ZONE BORNEO

DROP ZONE BORNEO

The RAF Campaign 1963–65

Roger Annett

Pen & Sword
AVIATION

First published in Great Britain in 2006 by
Pen & Sword Aviation
an imprint of
Pen & Sword Books Ltd
47 Church Street
Barnsley
South Yorkshire
S70 2AS

ISBN 1-84415-396-7

A CIP catalogue record for this book is
available from the British Library.

Typeset in 10/12 Times New Roman by
Concept, Huddersfield, West Yorkshire

Printed and bound in England by Biddles

Pen & Sword Books Ltd incorporates the Imprints of Pen & Sword Aviation,
Pen & Sword Maritime, Pen & Sword Military, Wharncliffe Local History,
Pen & Sword Select, Pen & Sword Military Classics and Leo Cooper.

For a complete list of Pen & Sword titles please contact
PEN & SWORD BOOKS LIMITED
47 Church Street, Barnsley, South Yorkshire, S70 2AS, England
E-mail: enquiries@pen-and-sword.co.uk
Website: www.pen-and-sword.co.uk

Contents

Acknowledgements

My thanks go to the many people whose contributions, insights and unfailing encouragement were generously offered during the preparation of this story.

Tom Sneddon painstakingly read the manuscript, correcting factual howlers and allowing free access to his own notes and records. These included selections from his letters home from the Far East, discovered in a box in his late mother's attic. Barry and Dorothy Priest's loft yielded equally priceless souvenirs and Mike Keane, a Changi Kiwi, produced the splendid Sarawak navigation chart. Both Dominic Parkinson and Dickie Miller unearthed valuable video footage (originally cine film) of the Confrontation years.

I am greatly indebted to Tony Stephens, recently Deputy Head at the Air Historical Branch. Here, Seb Cox, Flight Lieutenant Mary Hudson and Clive Richards gave me every assistance among the RAF Report Forms 540 and bundles of photographs. Tony also referred me to Henry Probert, whose advice was invaluable.

John Leary was a guide and mentor, not least among the RAF aviation accounts found in back-numbers of *Air Clues* at the RAF Museum at Hendon. He reintroduced me to Tony Talbot-Williams, to whom I am grateful for his helpful cooperation.

Geoff Walker, John Horsfall and Taff Howell put me in touch with old 215 Squadron friends from Borneo days: Pat Gorman, Jack Davies, John Hare, Tommy Norcross, Graham Wade, Mike Robson, Rod Twitchett and Jack Ord all gladly shared their recollections, as did Val McCarthy, Terry Keats and Hugh Rolfe from other squadrons.

I am grateful to Roger Draper for his part in initiating this project and to Celia Kent for her professional counsel and an introduction to Lord Healey, who kindly gave his ministerial viewpoint.

My foremost thanks go to my wife, Jenny, for her inestimable contribution to the writing and editing of this book. Without her, the tale would not have been told.

Roger Annett
Spring 2006

Foreword

This excellent book recalls how the Argosy aircraft of 215 Squadron took part in the 'Confrontation' with Indonesia in Borneo, which Denis Healey, Secretary of State for Defence at the time, rightly claims as one of the most efficient uses of military force in history. In this campaign, faced with organised infiltration by a larger neighbour into a country of dense jungle and few roads, deployment of troops by air and their resupply by airdrops was the only answer.

Great credit is due to the aircrews of 52 Squadron (Valettas), 48 Squadron (Hastings), 34 Squadron (Beverleys) and 41 Squadron RNZAF (Bristol Freighters), as well as the Argosies of 215 Squadron, who transported and resupplied the ground forces using aircraft that were not always ideal for the task. The RAF wanted the C-130 Hercules, but an understandable desire to 'Buy British' resulted in the Argosy, a civil aircraft designed to be a short-range European capital city 'packet', being modified for medium-range freight-carrying and military airdrop use.

Nevertheless, the opportunity to reform 215 squadron, with its gallant history from previous incarnations, to operate the new aircraft and to deploy to the Far East where military action was taking place, was grasped enthusiastically by air and groundcrews. The aircrews were drawn from experienced tactical transporters (including some splendid air quartermasters), four-engined aircraft pilots and navigators from Coastal and Bomber Commands, and a valuable group of keen, young aviators. These were backed up superbly by a groundcrew of similar mix.

On a visit to Singapore two months before deployment, to brief the Far East Air Force Headquarters air staff on the aircraft and its capability, I reported, 'No one in their right mind would have bought these aircraft, but the air and groundcrews will ensure that they are flown to their limit and perform all the operational tasks allotted to them.'

And so it proved to be. After a ten-leg transit the squadron operated within forty-eight hours of arrival at Changi. From then on the excellent performance on all tasks, in spite of very difficult Drop Zones (DZs), the limitations of the aircraft and cartography, is of great credit to all personnel.

This book will convey a picture of dedication, excitement, fear, frustration, fun and comradeship, which made the RAF such a worthwhile career. My time with 215 Squadron was certainly the highlight of mine, and with this book I have relived it.

Tony Talbot-Williams
Formerly Wing Commander RAF
Officer Commanding 215 Squadron

Preface

Our victory in Borneo is still too little known in Britain. In my memoir, *The Time of My Life*, I describe our operations in Confrontation – our struggle against the Indonesian invaders – as the most successful use of armed force in the twentieth century. After nearly four years of fighting, the toll of British casualties was no larger than that on the roads in Britain on a single Bank Holiday weekend.

The bulk of the fighting was done by Gurkha battalions and Britain's own special forces – the SAS and SBS. Britain's Director of Operations was General Walter Walker, who was himself a Gurkha General. He knew that our success depended on winning the hearts and minds of the local population, writing later: 'It was indelibly inscribed on our minds that one civilian killed by us would do more harm than ten killed by the enemy.'

I strongly agreed. When the RAF Commander in Singapore asked me for permission to bomb the Indonesian ports of entry in Eastern Borneo, I refused. At a time when the United States was plastering Vietnam with bombs, napalm and defoliant, leading disastrously to the death of millions of civilians and ultimate defeat, no British aircraft ever made an offensive strike in Borneo.

On the other hand, when Walker asked me to allow our forces to cross the border so as to ambush the enemy soldiers before they could enter Malaysian territory, I gave them permission under strict control. So I allowed the border crossings, first for small groups up to three thousand yards, and later for up to ten thousand yards with large bodies of men. The operations, code-named 'Claret', remained secret until long after Confrontation was over.

The role of the RAF was vital not only in providing the helicopters to ferry our troops into the jungle, but also to drop supplies to them. As this book describes most clearly, the dangers our supply aircraft faced over the Borneo jungles and mountains, and from the weather, were daunting; but the aircrews flew to success in their essential task.

Denis Healey
The Right Honourable Lord Healey of Riddlesden CH MBE
Secretary of State for Defence 1964–70

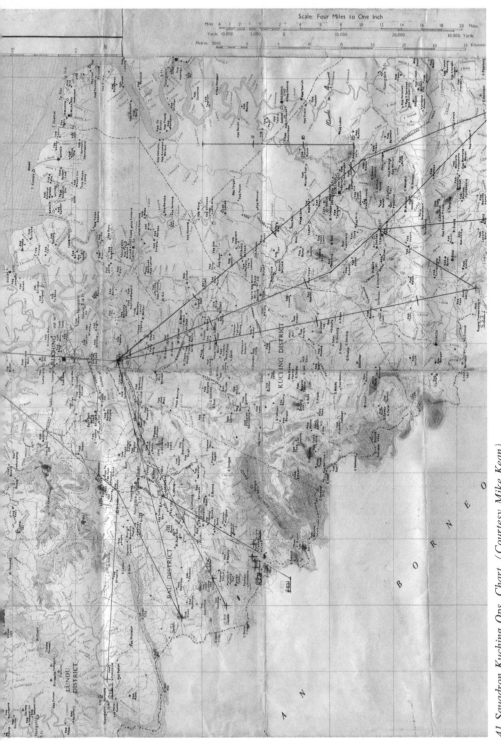

Scale: Four Miles to One Inch

41 Squadron Kuching Ops. Chart. (Courtesy Mike Kean)

CHAPTER ONE

Mission to the Mountains

O n the island the early morning air is cool and still, and the blue horizon is streaked with gold. The waters of the South China Sea lap gently onto the coral beach. Insects, birds and frogs call across the treetops and among the grasses. Against the lightening sky to the north-east rises the black shape of Kinabalu, a humpback mountain sacred to the tribes living in its shadow. The scent of frangipani is in the air – challenged by the smell of streaky bacon frying in the mess tent.

For this is a remote airbase of the British Far East Air Force on Labuan – some 50 square-miles of scrub, swamp and secondary jungle, lying 20 miles off the north-west coast of Borneo.

The equatorial sun rises fast, picking out the threatening shapes of warplanes – fighters, maritime patrol aircraft, helicopters and freighters. Today, one of the transports is tasked with carrying some 16,000 lb of military supplies 100 nautical miles into Borneo's unmapped mountain and jungle interior. There, its crew has to find three dropping zones each not much bigger than a cricket-pitch, and deliver this load by parachute to the British troops waiting on the ground.

The freighter is an Armstrong Whitworth Argosy, a twin-boom, high wing tactical transport, powered by four Rolls-Royce Dart MK 101 turbo-props. The RAF has eight of these aircraft stationed with 215 Squadron at Changi in Singapore, 800 miles to the west. Aircraft XR107 has made the four-hour flight out to Labuan, ready to begin a ten-day detachment – the first for the squadron in the Borneo Campaign.

It's the last week of October 1963. Deep in the central highlands, units of the British Army – the Royal Leicester Regiment, the Gurkhas and the SAS – supported by RAF helicopters, are holding down their sector of the thousand-mile border with Indonesian Kalimantan. Indonesian troops, together with the native tribes subverted to their cause, outnumber the

British and their allies by anything up to ten to one. They have Russian-built MiG fighters and Badger bombers, and lines of anti-aircraft batteries within sight of the border. They also have hostile intent.

This is another colonial conflict in the British pull-back from Empire and airdrops are a vital link in the supply chain. The troops and helicopter crews can't fight without their weekly delivery of fuel, foodstuffs and kit.

The military base lodges on the civilian airfield at Labuan, and the Airport Hotel serves as the Officers' Mess, with one room as temporary RAF Operations. At 0700 the Argosy's captain, navigator and co-pilot, in their light green, one-piece flying suits, walk along the verandah in the dawn light for flight-planning.

An Army Intelligence Officer briefs them on the enemy's activities. There's concern that the Indonesians plan to launch an attack down the rivers from the highlands to the coast, with oil-rich Brunei as the target. SAS patrols working right up on the front line have reports from the natives of increased enemy incursions and subversions.

The Allied Director of Operations, Major General Walter Walker, has ordered a strengthening of forces on this sector, and 215 Squadron with its Argosies has been detached to Labuan to double the airdrop capacity, alongside the Beverley heavy transports already out here. Today's task is to airlift kerosene, howitzer shells and bullets, victuals and kit. And rum rations and rice for the Gurkhas.

The Met Officer briefs on the weather conditions expected today. October has been a wetter than average month in Labuan, with twenty inches of rain to date. At this time of year, the rain comes in regular afternoon storms, when winds can gust up to 40 miles-per-hour. Over in Borneo, tropical mists will now be filling the jungle valleys of the target area. In an hour or so, the equatorial sun will be high enough to stir up the mists into cumulus clouds, shrouding the peaks. In the afternoon there'll be ferocious thunderstorms, unstable masses of overheated air that can tower above 30,000 feet and lift an aircraft 1,000 feet in a few seconds. The morning mission is therefore timed at 0930 to arrive in the mountains after the mists and before the storms.

The captain and navigator tackle the tricky business of finding today's dropping zones – the DZs. RAF Beverley transport crews are old hands at supply-dropping operations here and are ready to share their local knowledge, but this is the first try by 215 Squadron in the Argosy. Today's three DZs lie in the highest and most rugged part of the spinal range that marks the border of British Borneo. The Army has given grid references, but much of the land is unsurveyed, and the maps are primitive and often inaccurate. The navigator and co-pilot rule in the flight paths and measure the time and distance to the targets. They trust for the rest to the Argosy's magic navigation aid, Doppler-shift radar – and to the Mark 1 eyeball. Briefing done, the three officers make their way to breakfast – bacon butties and tea.

The captain is Squadron Leader John Leary, a Flight Commander on 215 Squadron, and he's no air-supply novice. Already, he has an operational tour on Beverleys under his belt, with detachments in Africa and the Middle East in a wide variety of terrain. Also, he has taken the trouble to recce today's DZs on one of those Beverleys, so he's calmly confident.

Flight Lieutenant Redvers 'Rev' Wilkins is the navigator, an experienced campaigner from maritime reconnaissance and anti-submarine duties in Cornwall but brand-new to the tropics and tactical transport. Like the skipper, he's a married man on a three-year tour in Changi, with his wife and family safe in the care of the all-providing British Sovereign Base of Singapore. He's mildly apprehensive.

The co-pilot is a Flying Officer, fresh from flying training via the Operational Conversion Unit (OCU) on the south coast of England. He has no more than fifty flying-hours on the Argosy and his supply-dropping experience is limited to two training sorties at Kuantan on the Malayan mainland. A single man, but with a promising new romance back in Changi, he's anxious but excited about this airdrop adventure. This is after all, what he joined up for.

At 0830 the officers collect flight kit, maps, manuals and nerves and in the bright sunlight, set out across the apron.

The Argosy shares its dispersal with a civilian Dakota airliner and an array of other RAF aircraft: a massive, double-decker Beverley and Single and Twin Pioneer short-field light transports. More sinister are the maritime patrol Shackletons bristling with aerials, and the three Hunter fighters for controlling the air where the freighters fly.

There's a sense of shared ownership as the fliers approach their Argosy. An aeroplane is no more than a hunk of riveted metal, wire, rubber and perspex, but away from home base, there's more than the usual close attachment. It's yours, it's vital, and you look after it. All three circle the airframe, checking that everything is in order: no popping rivets or unlocked panels, no loose or bent aerials, no cuts in the tyres and no oil or fuel leaks.

The other members of the crew have been out with the aircraft for an hour. The flight engineer is Warrant Officer Howarth, a man with many years of service and flying-hours dating from the Second World War and the 1948 Berlin Airlift. He has checked the work of the six airmen ground-crew who have serviced the machine overnight and refilled the fuel tanks with 3,300 gallons of kerosene. In these early days of the campaign they sleep when they can, in empty engine-boxes from the Beverleys, right out on the flight dispersal. They're a cheerful bunch, and just as well – they must work hard and faultlessly, on long shifts in harsh tropical conditions.

The air quartermaster (AQM), Colin Bateman, is young but already a full Sergeant. Volunteering for air dispatch duties puts a recruit on a fast track to NCO rank – and his youth earns a lot of ribbing from the hoarier members of the Sergeants' Mess. He has reported to the aircraft two hours before take-off to check loading – vital calculations to make sure that the heavy and varied stores don't disturb the aircraft trim. On route trips he serves meals to the crew and passengers on pink plastic trays, but today he's to work as dispatcher with a team of four muscular squaddies from No. 3 Army Air Service Operations of the Royal Army Service Corps (RASC).

Also volunteers for the job, they've already fork-lifted and manhandled eight 1-ton containers into the freight compartment of the Argosy through the gaping clam-shell doors at the rear. As they climb up into the belly through the hatch under the nose, the crew can see these hulking shapes filling the aircraft. Each stands some 4-feet-cubed on wooden pallets, swathed in netting and with the humped pack of a 40-feet diameter parachute on top. Six of these contain four 42-gallon drums of helicopter fuel and they're treated with great respect. The other two carry ammunition, clothing and food – and barrels of rum, a perk that the Gurkhas share with the Navy. The load is completed with a dozen sacks of rice. These supplies have been freighted out to Labuan in RAF aircraft and Royal Navy ships and they're now chained to the Argosy's roller floor.

The co-pilot follows 'Boss' Leary's black leather shoes up the ladder from the freight cabin to the flight deck. The smell up here is unique – a mixture of hot wiring, leather, oil and sweat. It's already hot and humid. The sun beats through the Perspex windshield and there's no air-conditioning. The temperature on the ground is climbing, there's no breeze and it'll be 90 degrees by midday. Humidity is above 80 per cent and cotton and polyester flying suits quickly become damp, then wet. The crew's keen to get up in the air and feel the fresher draught through the cabin.

They take station. 'Mister' Howarth is already there in position alongside his controls for the engines, electrics and hydraulics on the starboard cockpit wall. His swivel seat lets him line up facing forward between the pilots when needed, in touch with the throttles, fuel cocks, and the entire instrumentation under the cockpit roof. Facing aft at his plotting table with navigation aids racked up the rear cockpit bulkhead, Rev is on another swivel seat.

The co-pilot has the right-hand seat. He takes all his orders from the captain and handles the controls only when instructed, but he has prime responsibility for the radios. He's made a neat log on a clipboard with a note of today's air-traffic and emergency frequencies.

This then, will be their operating environment for an estimated three hours. Intercom and headsets on, harnesses fastened, the captain calls for pre-start-up checks. The navigator holds the list and calls the cues.

Power is already on, provided by the squat box of a mobile diesel generator plugged into the nose. The disembodied voice of the ground-crew chief comes on the line. Fuel levels, fire-warning systems, outside air temperatures – all are checked. The co-pilot is instructed to switch on the radios – UHF for contact with Labuan Air Traffic Control and VHF for use across Borneo.

On command, he transmits: 'Permission to start engines.'

Labuan local responds: 'Clear to start.'

The captain and engineer play their toccatas on the switches and levers and one by one the four Rolls-Royces on the wings begin their stately rotation. Near-paraffin fuel is squirted into the combustion chambers and ignited, and a continuous controlled explosion drives the turbine, which spins the prop, which pulls in the air, which mixes with the fuel – non-stop for hours. The men on board know they are great engines for reliability, but they could do with a bit more power at this weight and in this heat – and at the altitude of the coming airdrop in the mountains. The props spin faster, their racket shattering the morning calm.

The instructions continue: 'Air Quartermaster, dispatch team strap in. Co-pilot, permission to taxi.'

The skipper waves away the wheel chocks, and as he opens the throttles and releases the brakes, the heavily laden freighter eases reluctantly forwards. He checks the brakes and the aeroplane dips its nose in response before waddling and bumping across the uneven concrete dispersal area. The whole airframe trembles. The distinctive thrum of the turboprops beats across the airbase – an exhilarating call to action.

One hand on the nose-steering wheel, one on the throttles, the Boss coaxes the ship across the dispersal. Threading the 115 feet of wingspan through the closely parked aircraft is a tricky business – but the 36-feet turning circle helps. The co-pilot watches the starboard wing tip and the sights of the Labuan base as they slip by: *basha* huts, wood-tiled roofs on Shell Oil's Membedai Club, lines of tents, swimming beaches – one for officers and one for non-commissioned ranks – the Control Tower and the approaching runway and take-off point.

On the horizon loom the distant bulk of Kinabalu and the mountains of Borneo – the day's destination.

Two thousand yards of fine concrete runway is the reason Labuan has become the main RAF base in Borneo. The aircraft backtracks down to the southern end by the seashore, wheels 180 degrees around and lines up, with the nose wheel over the centre line.

With the hand-brake on, the captain calls for pre-take-off checks. Flaps are lowered 10 degrees, the power-boosting water-methanol pumps are set to stand-by, the lock is released and the flying controls are swung through their full travel, making sure that the elevators, rudders and ailerons are free and smooth.

'Permission to take off' – from the Tower.

The captain moves the throttle levers firmly forward, the props spin up to 15,000 revolutions per minute, water-methanol supercharging cuts in and the engine note is a full-throated roar. Temperatures and pressures are checked as the airframe heaves and struggles against the brakes.

Gripping the control column, the captain calls to the co-pilot, 'You have the throttles.'

At 0930 precisely the brakes are off and the Argosy surges forward, now kept straight with the rudders.

'V1' – committed to take off now.

'VR' – rotate. Control column back and at 110 knots the 100,000 lb of metal, rivets, fuel and cargo lifts massively into the air.

'V2' – safety speed for climbing away.

After take-off checks are completed: 'Undercarriage up' – at 50 feet.

'Water-meth off.' The limit for water-methanol boosting is thirty seconds.

'Flaps up,' at 400 feet.

'Revs back to fourteen five hundred.' This is for the climb.

The engine noise is now a symphony of four pitches as the props struggle to synchronise, sending shudders through the airframe. The Argosy climbs in a shallow turn across the island, speed building to 150 knots, and the take-off panorama unfolds – for the co-pilot, a wonder every time.

Labuan airbase is now fully awake. A fighter moves to begin its border patrol, helicopter rotors are turning and the Dakota is taxiing for its morning schedule to Kota Kinabalu – still marked on the chart with its colonial name Jesselton – over the sea and under the slopes of the great mountain.

On course for the highlands, 10 degrees east of south, the co-pilot transfers to Approach Control. On the VHF he has set the international air distress frequency just to listen out for any trouble – he hopes to God he'll not have to shout for help himself.

Climbing over Brunei Bay, the coast of Sarawak is a few miles ahead, still under a veil of low cloud. The Joint Headquarters of the British forces and their allies are in Brunei town and an RAF Pembroke communications aircraft is on the approach below, ferrying staff officers to and from Labuan.

'Coasting into Sarawak,' is the radio call to Labuan Control and XR107 is now over the main landmass of Borneo – at 300,000 square miles, one of the largest islands in the world.

Through breaks in the cloud, the land below has the look of the well-grassed downlands of Sussex and Kent. But the co-pilot knows it's virgin tropical forest with trees up to 300 feet high, massed closely together for hundreds and hundreds of miles.

Navigation over these jungles isn't easy. Great expanses of the chart – recently published – have no contours, just rivers and some spot heights. But even these can't be relied on. A note informs: *This map is not an authority on international boundaries.* That could be quite interesting with the Indonesian border forming the front-line.

The first DZ is about 50 nautical miles away now – twenty minutes' flying time – and the Argosy will climb to 8,000 feet. Is this a safe height for this leg? The manual says drily: *Safety height gives clearance over known high ground, particularly important in cloudy or hazy conditions.* The snag is that in Borneo, the exact height of the ground is often not known.

The co-pilot has no experience yet in finding the way by ground features. But the navigator uses the Doppler radar to check track and distance, and on the time reckoned for the leg, the whole crew will look out for the DZ – the village and base at Long Semado.

They can pick out the muddy, meandering thread of the Trusan River, the main artery up to the central highlands on the Sarawak side. Here and there are tiny longhouse villages on its banks. The co-pilot marks them on his chart and notes the occasional sandbank in the river for possible last-ditch crash-landing areas.

At cruising height, the skipper trims the aircraft to straight and level, and there's a new engine note as the constant-speed props adjust to 200 knots. The engineer works his magic on the synchronisation switches and lessens the thrum in the eardrums.

To port, the pilots can see the slopes of Batu Binuda rising to 8,000 feet just over the border in Sabah. It stands clear of the valley mists – a landmark that is in the right place on the chart and one that can't be missed. In cloud, it's one to be avoided.

The Doppler tells them they're nearly there so it's all eyes peeled. The map says that Long Semado lies up a steep river valley and no more than 8 miles from Indonesian Kalimantan.

The Boss spots the target first, through a gap in the cloud and valley mists now just beginning to vaporise in the tropical sun. The co-pilot looks from the jumble of peaks all around down to the village below, with its short dirt airstrip, almost invisible in the never-ending jungle.

The flight deck springs into action. The captain calls: 'Power back to nine thousand,' and at 150 knots begins a left-hand circling descent through the gap in the cloud into the valley below.

'Flaps to approach please, Co.'

The 24 degrees of flap drop the aircraft's nose, giving a steeper flight path and better visibility. The Argosy descends gingerly above the mountain slopes, both pilots ever alert to potential downstream escape routes. An upstream valley could turn into a one-way death-trap.

With his charts and headset, Rev makes his way down the ladder to take up his airdrop position, prone at the supply-aimer's window in the aircraft's nose. AQM and dispatchers are called to readiness and each one attaches a lifeline to a cable running along the freight compartment walls.

On the descent, the captain and navigator get their bearings. Long Semado is on a bend in the river, a defence, so it's said, against any neighbouring tribes with lingering head-hunting ambitions. Helpfully, the DZ is marked with two white letters, laid out on the airstrip. On the far bank, it's not much longer than a football pitch and just 50 feet wide.

Down in the valley, with the village to starboard, the skipper sets up a tight left-hand circuit at what he reckons to be 1,500 feet above the ground. There's a radio altimeter but it's not to be trusted over these hills.

The co-pilot watches the villagers scurrying about below, disturbed by this strange silver monster whistling around in the cloud above the trees. There are no soldiers in sight – probably staying under cover in case of a surprise Indonesian strike. The border is very close and it's all too easy to picture lines of Indonesian machine-guns over those ridges. But as the Argosy flies across the river, a green flare soars up from the jungle. The troops are there and it's all clear to drop.

The captain turns in for a first pass, letting down to 700 feet – and calls for power to maintain a speed of 115 to 120 knots. This gives the engines to the flight engineer who plays the throttle and fuel levers forward and back with the props howling in response. The navigator looks for an airrelease point allowing for height, wind and speed, and the weight of the stores. He picks a landmark that he'll recognise on the next run-in – an isolated plot cultivated by the young women of the village. The co-pilot's attention is held for a moment by the girls – it's his first sight of the fabled natives of Borneo.

The Argosy is now over the DZ. It seems a bit bigger from down here so there should be room for any small error with the containers. Undershoot and they're in the jungle and most likely lost for ever – overshoot and the containers pitch into the flooded river and might be washed miles downstream.

Through patches of mist, the aircraft clambers back over the hills. At the end of the circuit, it slips down again for the first live run: dropping down – steadying up – watching the speed.

Below 120 knots it's safe to open the rear clam-shell doors. The order is given and the AQM downstairs pulls the switch. As they open, there's a change in the airflow and an additional rumble from the shuddering airframe.

The dispatchers group around the four 1-ton containers of kerosene that they'll soon be hauling across the floor rollers and out into the slipstream. They're strong-nerved guys – they need to be.

The Argosy plunges across the jungle canopy rising and falling steeply below. Hugging the mountain slope to starboard, it turns for a run of half a mile or so – just fifteen to twenty seconds straight and level to make each drop. The smoke from the village fires shows that the surface wind is light so the 'chutes should fall with little drift.

From the nose, the navigator calls the directions: 'Right a bit – left a bit – steady.'

The engineer plays his tunes on the engines, maintaining speed. The captain grips the controls. The co-pilot watches the trees and hills, scanning the horizon for those MiGs.

'Left a bit – steady – red light on!'

The dispatchers lean back against the first 1-ton container, pull out the fixing pins and then take the weight, two each side, holding the container by brute strength alone.

At the aiming point: 'Green light on!'

Straining every muscle, they heave the container towards the green expanse below. With a rumble on the rollers and a heavy thump over the lower sill, it's cast into the void, taking its own chances now. There's a thwack from the static line hitched to the upper clam-shell door, a snap as the parachute's dragged from its bag, and a cracking slap from the opening 'chute. They stumble back into the safety of the freight cabin, hauling in the static line and flapping parachute bag.

'Load gone – doors closing,' calls the AQM.

'Full power,' orders the captain and away they go and round again.

Bravely perched on the closing lower sill, Sergeant Bateman watches the 'chute and container swaying down to the DZ below, ready to relay the good or bad news. Has the load of kerosene found its way down to the waiting soldiers? Or into oblivion, lost in the primary jungle or the depths of the river? Please God, not into the longhouses.

'Twenty yards at nine o'clock,' comes the triumphant news. The load's right on the edge of the DZ but it's there. One down, three to go.

So it's round on a tight left-hand circuit while the next container is rolled back to the doors. Letting down to dropping height, in goes the freighter again, engines wailing and doors opening.

The navigator uses the same aiming point but brings the aircraft in a bit further to the right.

'Green light on!'

And away it goes, right on target. The white 'chutes make good sighters now and the final two 1-ton containers land safely alongside the others. With full power, building up speed, the aircraft swoops over the DZ once more to give Rev time to clamber back upstairs and reset the Doppler. The skipper dips each wing to salute the natives and troops still under cover on the ground, and lifts the Argosy over the mist and the mountains. The crew is pleased – the delivery boys have done their stuff. The co-pilot, with his first taste of the action, is starting to get an idea of what it's all about.

The climb is steeper with half the load gone, as the course is set for Ba Kelalan, another village just 20 nautical miles south of Long Semado at about the same altitude. The chart shows it just 2 miles from the Indonesian frontier – worryingly near. In the foothills of the high border range, this DZ needs to be approached with an even closer watch on safe heights and escape routes. At least the mist is now almost gone. There are two 1-ton containers to deliver here, much-needed fuel for the helicopters supporting the SAS jungle patrols.

Ba Kelalan turns out to be a real bitch of a DZ. It's a much smaller strip, again by a river, and the valley slopes are steep. After two hazardous and terrifying attempts uphill, the Boss goes for the slightly less risky downhill flight path, but even then the aircraft has to be squeezed right up against a ridge – the border ridge – on final approach. The co-pilot reckons Indonesian gunners could even now be setting their sights.

Throttled back with flaps down, the aeroplane skims the trees on the wing tip, bellies down into the river valley and finds just enough straight and level to make a dropping run. The navigator finds an aiming point and it's round for the real thing. With full power, the captain makes a steep climbing turn to starboard to clear the hills and get back to circuit height. He'd better get it right – too tight a turn and there's a real danger of stalling. And after the throttles are opened, the turboprops take a frightening moment or two to pick up power. Fists gripping the leather armrests, the co-pilot stares out at the wooded slopes filling the windscreen from side to side.

It's bumpy down here. The sun has boiled up a stew of treetop thermals and the aeroplane is flexing. The Argosy, with its twin-booms, cavernous fuselage and high-wing props, each the length of two tall men, gives a shuddering ride even in light cloud. Fully laden in the wind-shears of Borneo, it's gut-wrenching. The courage of the men at the open doors downstairs – swaying on their straps with the props beating against their ears – is beyond belief.

At the controls, the skipper loosens his damp collar and Rev at the lower window mutters to himself in the midst of the racket around him. Sergeant Bateman and the dispatchers gape at the treetops just outside the doors. Were those gibbons swinging through the branches? Mister Howarth has seen it all before, but the co-pilot has never been at the limits like this. He sits transfixed, with the mountainside at his elbow. His flying suit sticks to his back and the flight deck stinks with nervous sweat.

'Green light on!'

The command has never been more welcome. The dispatchers heave out the 1-ton container and the captain goes again into a full power water-methanol-boosted climb-away and racking right-hand turn back to circuit height. Downwind, the crew can see the container and 'chute right by the ident letter. Can they do it again?

They can. It's hot and it's hell but their skills are sharpened and maybe the gods are with them.

There's no third run to reset the Doppler – the threat from the border ridge is too real. With the doors closed and flaps raised, the lightened Argosy barrels back along the river valley. His hands shaking, the co-pilot fumbles for his cigarettes. What the hell's coming next?

Just under two hours from take-off the crew steels itself for the final DZ of the morning – Bario.

Bario is another 20 nautical miles to the south-south-west, and the co-pilot's chart shows it on one of the few flat grassland areas of the Borneo highlands – the Plain of Bah. It's less than ten minutes' flying time in a straight line but Mount Murud rules out that course. The crags of this mighty mountain soar at 8,000 feet, above the clouds and bang on track. To port, lies the Indonesian border just 10 miles away and to starboard there are two more high mountains in a line: Batu Lawi – its twin white peaks a great landmark – and Batu Iran. The co-pilot is beginning to fix a pattern of the landscape in his brain. The Doppler's working a treat and the aircraft is at least 10,000 lb lighter so it's possible to go over the mountains. But consulting with the navigator, the skipper opts to fly the long way round Mount Murud, across the 50-mile Tamabo ridge further south, then back up over the plain to Bario.

The co-pilot reckons he's as game as anyone, but all the same, he's glad they're not going to push their luck. The captain has the controls, the engineer the systems and the navigator all sorts to do both *en route* and over the DZs. But apart from the occasional radio call and the flap lever to set, the co-pilot's job is to sit with gritted teeth and watch the non-stop action. He really could use a little less excitement for a while.

The autopilot is engaged, the engines are synchronised and all proceeds as planned. The dispatchers relax downstairs with a cuppa from the galley. The smiling head of Sergeant Bateman appears through the flight-deck hatch, and steady as a rock he balances a tray of coffee and digestives on one hand. It seems that for him, it's just another day at the office.

It's now late-morning and the promised cumulus clouds are building above the steamy valleys and mountain slopes. These clouds are lumpy, either with turbulence (very uncomfortable), or with concealed granite crags (positively fatal). The co-pilot is seriously grateful for XR107's Cloud and Collision Warning Radar (CCWR).

The Argosy snakes through the peaks and finds Bario, mercifully clear of mist and cloud. The village longhouse sits on a small hill alongside a grass airstrip, marked as the spot to drop. Nearby, the Gurkhas have set up base to guard against Indonesian insurgents. The co-pilot has heard about Bario and its role as a centre of operations for Allied third-columnists against the Japanese in 1944 and 1945. They and the native Kelabits built the airstrip, the first in Borneo outside the main towns. He's aware, too, that there was a major action here just a few weeks ago when RAF Twin Pioneers flew in fifty Greenjackets to drive insurgents back over the border. The Intelligence Officer has warned of small-arms fire.

Bario turns out to be a friendly DZ, much less threatened by encircling mountain slopes. But the limestone crags of the Tamabo mountains 2 miles to the west provide a spectacular backdrop and encourage a fairly tight circuit, as does the border not far distant to the east.

The final two 1-ton containers, the essential weekly consignment of clothes, food, ammunition – and rum – are dropped neatly in the middle of the strip. But the bags of rice mean a free-drop.

The Boss has done this before but it's another eye-opener for the co-pilot. The bags are double-skinned and are heaved out of the side doors of the Argosy at 105 knots. The idea is that on impact, only one of the bags breaks, leaving the other to protect the stores – soft goods like rice, flour, or cement. For this to work, the bags – according to operating instructions – need to be dropped from a height ... *not above 50 feet.* Judging that 50 feet – less than half the height of Nelson's Column – is quite a trick. He's heard it said that at least once in training, a 12-inch radio aerial under the aircraft belly has accidentally served as a lower limit guide.

But today, the aircraft eases down over a run-in long enough to get a steady straight and level. The air is calm and all goes well – three bullseyes in a row.

Swooping down over the jungle scrub and long grasses, under the longhouse up on the hill, the Argosy is almost level with the rice huts and wide-eyed, bare-breasted native girls in the *padi* fields. These must be the maidens who, in Officers' Mess bar stories, welcome the RAF Gods from the Sky in their great silver birds. The co-pilot believes these tales and makes plans to hitch a lift some day in a silver bird that can actually land here – a helicopter or a Pioneer. For now, he has to be content with just a fleeting impression of this wonderful place high on the spine of Borneo.

The aircraft climbs away and circles for height – not too much, the border's on that ridge. The navigator on the CCWR gets them round the worst of the clag over the Tamabo range but there's still plenty of the stuff to plough through. Lurching around the sky, the freighter avoids the crags and, clear of the peaks, heads for Labuan. The AQM and dispatchers tidy up downstairs, securing straps, chains and parachute bags, and in the cockpit the autopilot is engaged for the cruise back to base.

The co-pilot is gazing out at the spectacular cloudscapes, reliving the morning, when the captain's voice breaks into his thoughts.

'Co, you have control – your approach and landing.'

'Roger, Skipper – I have control.' He hopes he sounds cool – he feels far from it. Here he is among the Big Boys, asked to fly the aircraft into Labuan. He sits up straight and considers his actions. His first is to hand the radio log across to the captain – captains enjoy having a go on the radios – and then to ask the navigator for confirmation of the course and ETA for landing.

'Zero-two-zero magnetic and forty minutes past midday.' The response is immediate and confident.

Rev's professional calm is reassuring, as are the experience of Mister Howarth and the watchful eye of the Boss. He mustn't foul up this first 215 Squadron airdrop mission – it must finish in style. There should be nothing to it – he's landed it dozens of times before – but never at Labuan on a tropical midday with four soldiers downstairs. Added to that, there could be quite a bit of traffic, including those pesky helicopters buzzing about. But he's done the training so he should be ready.

He scans the instruments: height 8,000 feet, speed 220 knots, engines at cruising revs and autopilot engaged. He looks out of the window for orientation. They're clear of cloud now and to starboard stand those landmark twin peaks of Batu Lawi, which means that further over there is

Long Semado, the first DZ this morning. So it must be about time to start the descent.

'Top of descent, Nav?'

'In two minutes, Co.' That's two minutes for further orientation and a re-cap of procedures.

To the north-east are the rugged ranges leading up to Kinabalu with its halo of cloud. To port are the oilfields of Brunei and the villages of the Sea Dyaks. Ahead lies home base, the paradise island of Labuan, shielded to the east by miles of impenetrable mangrove swamps on the coast of Brunei Bay.

And the procedures? First, the top-of-descent checks. He should ask the skipper to call Labuan approach control with position and ETA. With the autopilot switches, he eases the nose down using the trim wheel to balance the elevators.

He calls the AQM with the ETA – they're now twenty minutes away. He lets the speed build up to above 250 knots, still with cruising power for maximum efficiency. The aim is to level out at 2,000 feet, 10 miles out for the approach, joining a left-hand circuit overhead at 1,200 feet. Just like that. He scans the instruments and the horizon as the aeroplane enters what is statistically, despite all that excitement in the mountains, the most hazardous stage of the mission – approach and landing.

A crackle in the headset.

'One-zero-seven, you are clear for straight-in approach. Call Labuan local. Over.'

The captain acknowledges. It's good news – it takes five minutes less. But it means coming in over a runway threshold just 50 yards from the shore, judging height, speed and power on a steady glide-path. It's a one-shot thing – exposed and with no margin for error.

He needs to get the speed back now. He calls for 10,000 revs from the engineer. He'd better try flying this thing. Feet on the rudder-bar and hands on the column, he disconnects the autopilot. The aircraft accepts his command. He's in control now.

Procedures continue: bringing the speed back to 150 knots, calling for approach flap and keeping a good look-out for other traffic.

Rev, God bless him, suggests the airfield approach checks. Mister Howarth, God bless him too, confirms fuel sufficient and all systems in order. The height's now 2,000 feet, speed 120 knots, 10 miles to run. The air in the cabin is getting hot and sticky again and inside the stained shammy-leather flying gloves his hands are clammy.

'Air Quartermaster, four minutes to landing. Strap in.'

Downstairs, the dispatchers, dozing on the parachute bags, are harried into their bum-bruising canvas sling seats.

'Landing-checks please, Nav.'

Speed's now below 120 knots: 'Undercarriage down.'

The skipper pushes the button. Three red lights glow on the under-carriage indicator and then after three healthy clunks from under the nose and wings, three welcome greens.

'Water-meth pumps on.' This is in case of having to overshoot and go round again.

'Permission to land.' Granted – there is nothing else in the circuit. It must be lunchtime.

Damn, the speed's too high – ease the nose up. Now the glide-path's too high – pull power back. That's better.

'Full flap.' Landing flap pitches the nose down, giving a great view of the shoreline and the runway approach. It's looking good.

The beach rushes up and the Argosy skims over the threshold. The co-pilot eases the control column back to round out and as the nose rises, the aircraft sinks towards the runway.

'Power off.'

The aircraft bumps onto the concrete with a screech and then a rumble from the tyres. After three-and-a-half hours' hard work, the mission has touched down.

'Props to fully fine.'

The prop-blades swivel to face the 90 miles-per-hour airstream. He hears again the fantastic engine roar and feels the tug of his harness as the braking props beat against the protesting air.

Made it! But he can't relax yet – he's still in charge of 50,000 lb of aircraft going like a train.

Try the brakes – gently. Keep straight with rudders – transfer to nose-wheel steering. Bring to a halt well short of the end of the landing strip. Turn the aircraft round on the runway with a bit of help from power and rudders.

He feels good – he always enjoys taxiing. The Argosy doesn't bloody well flex on the ground – it goes where it's pointed. And there's an audience – air traffic, other aircrew and the groundcrew waiting at dispersal.

He completes the after-landing checks: water-methanol pumps off – flaps up – control locks on. With props howling, the Argosy jolts back over the hardstanding to the parking point, following the hand signals of a marshalling airman. With the aircraft at a halt and the parking brake on, the rear doors are opened. The co-pilot signals to the handlers to slide in the chocks and closes down the engines, electrics and hydraulics. Blessed silence again. He draws a deep breath and lets it out slowly. His body relaxes and he climbs out of his harness.

The crew clambers down the ladder and out through the side doors, accessible now that the load has gone, safely delivered to the customers up-country. In the stifling heat, the captain hands the Argosy over to the groundcrew chief for servicing and refuelling, and to the Army for reloading. There's a second bullets and bully beef delivery to fly today.

There's no mention of the fears and tensions of the morning as the officers make their way to the Ops Room to debrief. Heartfelt relief at their safe return to base is disguised.

'Pretty good for a first go, Rev. Clean sheet. Must be all that practice you had lobbing depth-charges out of the Shack.'

'Thanks, Skip. You didn't do too bad yourself. Those close-ups of the girls at Bario were a nice surprise. And what do you think of young Lofty's performance? Don't think he took too much off the tyres.'

His skipper's nod of approval and broad grin tells the co-pilot what he wants to know. He's joined the Big Boys.

CHAPTER TWO

Into *Confrontasi*

The image is clear in my mind of that fair-haired, twenty-three-year-old Flying Officer – all six-foot-six of him – striding in the heat haze away from the Argosy. I recognise him as myself – but a very different man from the one standing at the bar in the Officers' Mess at RAF Uxbridge four decades later. My brother-in-law had invited me to a Dining-in Night, my first since becoming a civilian many years before.

'Wear your Borneo medal,' he said.

He had a Borneo medal too. I discovered after marrying his beautiful sister that he had been in Sarawak, at RAF Kuching, at about the same time as I was starting my tour out there. Rather self-consciously, I pinned the miniature to my dinner jacket and set off for what was to be a surprising evening.

We sat on opposite sides of a sprig surrounded by ridiculously young-looking Air Traffic Pilot Officers. Our General Service Medals with the Borneo clasp prompted a string of questions about the campaign.

When was it? What was it about? Who was the enemy? What was it like?

We gave them all the tales about the bugs and beasts, the heat and humidity and our adventures off and on the ground. We dined out on Borneo stories and didn't once put our hands in our pockets at the bar. More than once I heard, 'You should write it all down, Sir.'

I was moved by the young officers' enthusiastic interest in our exploits. On my way home I thought that if ever a story deserved to be told, it was this one – about the air-supply crews in that low profile and almost-forgotten campaign, fought out there in the Far East while Britain got on with the swinging sixties.

The Borneo campaign was dubbed the 'Indonesian Confrontation' and the roots of this undeclared war were long, and deep in the tribal and colonial conflicts of at least two centuries out in the spice islands of South East Asia. My airdrop crew was engaged in the kind of jungle campaigning begun in the Second World War in the mountains of Burma,

refined in the British occupation of Java and Sumatra in 1946 and continued in the twelve-year struggle against the Communists in the Malayan
Emergency of the 1950s. The whole campaign was arguably one of the
most successful uses of military force and air power in British history.

Why were we so involved in the domestic affairs of sovereign nations on
the other side of the world? Which were the squadrons, battalions and
flotillas? How did it all start?

The conflict got under way with the Brunei Rebellion.

On Monday 10 December 1962, a Beverley transport of 34 Squadron
RAF came skimming low across the waters of Brunei Bay, jam-packed
with soldiers of the Queen's Own Highlanders. In full combat kit, bristling
with weaponry, they were strapped to the four rows of sling-seats in the
freight-bay of that flying warehouse. It was a bumpy flight at low level and
breezy with the side fuselage doors removed – ready for a rapid and
aggressive exit. This force was tasked with liberating the Shell oil refinery
at Seria in the British protectorate of Brunei, just 70 nautical miles south-
west of Labuan.

The refinery had been captured two days before by 5,000 Indonesian-
inspired armed rebels, intent on overthrowing the benevolent but auto-
cratic rule of the Sultan. They were backed by the Brunei People's Party,
would-be Republicans who in the September governmental elections had
won all sixteen seats, only for the Sultan to appoint seventeen of his own
cronies to regain control. The rebels were incensed about that and also
about the proposed Federation of Malaysia which they saw as a front for
continued British Imperial ambitions.

The Sultan supported the Federation, which would unify the states of
Malaya and Singapore with the British Borneo colonies of North Borneo,
Sarawak and the protectorate of Brunei, to counter the territorial
ambitions of President Sukarno of Indonesia. Sukarno had in mind a
different federation – comprising all the proposed Malaysian states,
Indonesia and the Philippines. He was sure of his ground, for the USA
had supported his recent successful struggle against Dutch rule in the East
Indies and he reckoned the Americans would back him against Malaysia
and the British.

The Indonesians were spreading fierce anti-Malaysia and anti-British
propaganda throughout Brunei's 84,000 population and training a 2,000-
strong guerrilla force at bases not far over the border in Indonesian
Borneo, Kalimantan. In addition, about 8,000 Brunei locals had signed up
for the cause.

Oil as always, was an important factor and the Brunei rebels knew
that Sukarno had nationalised the Dutch Shell oilfields in Indonesia. The

great refinery at Seria was therefore a key strategic target. The rebels, about 95 per cent local people, had taken over most of the place, as well as the nearby airfield and police station, and were holding fifty or sixty European hostages.

Holed up in the control tower, they were armed with the shotguns given to them by the British in the struggle against Japanese occupation in the Second World War – and with half-a-dozen Indonesian machine-guns.

The airfield at Seria, a reinforced grass strip, was under water. The south-west monsoon had come early that year and 17 inches of rain in four days had fractured the main water main.

The Beverley was an awe-inspiring sight as it roared in over the sea-shore. An out-sized aircraft, its high wing carried four Bristol Centaurus internal-combustion engines, the biggest and noisiest that had ever flown. The full flap on its huge aerofoil and the mighty propellers churned the saturated tropical air into a ragged, swirling curtain. The pilot dropped the aircraft in from 10 feet to cut through the surface water and to get the shortest possible landing run. With the propellers pulled into reversed pitch, the airframe was enveloped in spray.

The rebels, seriously rattled, opened up with their machine-guns. As the aircraft slowed, the Highlanders hit the ground running, fanning out over the waterlogged airfield, every rifle with fixed bayonet and a bullet up the spout.

Without stopping, the Beverley captain shoved the props into forward gear and opened the throttles to full power. The aircraft had stopped half-a-dozen bullets but the powerful engines set the giant propellers spinning at full speed and the freighter thundered back into the air, just over one hundred seconds from landing.

The Highlanders advanced swiftly on the control tower and the rebel fire was silenced. Those guerrillas that could, fled to the cover of the trees, abandoning their machine-guns and their dead, wounded or captured comrades.

At the same time, on the other side of the refinery, five Twin Pioneers of 209 Squadron RAF were landing Gurkha troops on rough ground by the police station. It was a tight approach and the aircraft could only make it by clipping the boundary trees. One aircraft bogged down on landing, but its soldiers splashed across the sodden terrain and joined up with the rest, now moving towards the rebel-held buildings. The guerrillas were caught in a pincer movement and immobilised. Seria was cleared in two days and all the European hostages released.

Forty miles to the east, Brunei town had seen further action. The rebels had failed to secure the airfield and the Beverleys and Pioneers could ferry troops without coming under fire. Up-river in Limbang the Australian

Resident and his wife endured a harrowing three days as hostages before they were rescued by Marine Commandos. Some 5,000 rebels were rounded up and the revolt was over within ten days.

The Indonesians continued the diplomatic war against Malaysia. The Americans and the United Nations were inclined to support the Indonesian cause, but British diplomacy eventually won them round. The fierce propaganda broadcasts from Djakarta continued and in January 1963 President Sukarno named the struggle *Confrontasi*. Tempers flared, the Indonesians set up terrorist camps along the Sarawak and North Borneo borders, and armed incursions started. The British reinforced their garrisons and bases in Borneo.

At the time of the Brunei Rebellion, I was one of a bunch of young pilots installed at No. 5 Flying Training School at RAF Oakington near Cambridge.

My flying career began in the summer of 1957 over the fields and hills of Surrey in a dual-control de Havilland Tiger Moth. I was an enthusiastic member of the school cadet force and was put up for an RAF Flying Scholarship. In the spring I'd found myself at Pilot Selection at RAF Hornchurch, standing stark naked on one leg with my eyes closed (Balance), then listening to a series of electronic bleeps (Hearing), and operating a basic joystick and firing button machine (Coordination). In due course a letter arrived offering me thirty hours' instruction, leading to a Private Pilot's Licence.

Flying the Tiger – a fabric-covered biplane with an open cockpit and in-line piston engine – is a motorbike ride in the sky. There were a dozen of them, painted silver, all in a row at Fairoaks Flying Club. The instructors were ex-RAF and familiar with the airfield from when it was a wartime training base and relief fighter station. After six hours' basic instruction, we set off on my twelfth dual flight, hoping it would lead to my first solo. The ground-handler swung the wooden propeller and the throb of the Gipsy Major rocked the whole of the aeroplane. The airscrew drove heady fumes of petrol and hot oil into our nostrils, buffeted the fin and rudder and snatched at the controls. Taxiing was a bumpy affair on the grass airfield and the high nose had to be swung constantly from side to side using the rudder and tail skid. On take-off, the slipstream rose to a gale in our faces, and the little Tiger Moth lifted off at just 56 knots. The countryside, magically as always, fell away.

We flew off to the Hog's Back to practise stalls and spins. The stall in the Tiger Moth is sedate, but the spin's something else. With the throttle closed and the nose up, the point of the stall is approached in eerie silence. Just as the wings lose their lift, the left boot jams on full left rudder. With rigging wires singing and ailerons clattering, over comes the nose. The left wing drops with a lurch and the aircraft corkscrews down at an alarming rate. Right boot, and stick centrally forward bring the sickening spiral to a stop, and full power pulls the biplane through. It was during this exercise that I learnt to throw up over the left-hand side of the cockpit – the other way and the flow from the prop blows it back in your face.

On landing, we taxied back to the take-off point and all of a sudden the instructor was clambering out of the front cockpit.

'Off you go then. One circuit and landing – make it smooth.'

A clap on the shoulder and he was gone, to stand at the threshold with his seat cushions on his head – the rather comical signal to the other aircraft that there was a first solo on.

There was no point in hanging around. Take-off checks – clear on the approach – line up. The beat of the prop and its firm grip on the airframe settled the nerves. I was in control. Stick back – throttle open – temperatures and pressures within limits – goggled eyes peering along the shoulder of the fuselage – keeping straight with the rudder. Stick forward and tail up, off we flew. Me and this lovely old machine – solo.

I turned to port for a circuit, imagining all my course-mates watching intently, waiting for a mistake. In no time at all I was on the approach, gliding down with the prop idling and the rush of the slipstream through the bracing struts just louder than the putter-putter of the engine. Over the threshold the ground rushed up. Levelling out – stick right back – sliding in on three points. Perfect! Nothing to beat it.

I was hooked, and with my silver wings on my cadet uniform, abandoned the planned path to university and joined the RAF.

Following three whole years of officer and pilot training as cadets at the RAF College, Cranwell, half-a-dozen of us are posted as Pilot Officers to RAF Oakington for advanced flying training on the Vickers Varsity, a medium-sized aeroplane with twin piston engines. Patient instructors lead us through the mysteries of RPM and boost, crosswind landings and asymmetric flight. When the instructors judge us ready, we're sent off in pairs with packed lunches and flasks of coffee for cross-country flying along the canals and ditches of the East Anglian fens.

We now reckon ourselves pilots so it's high time to acquire motor cars. I hand over forty quid in fivers to a Jordanian pilot trainee and become the proud owner of a 1935 Morris 8 – as old as the Tiger Moth. Before the driving test I'm given advanced roundabout tuition on the A1 by one colleague, Val McCarthy, and another, Robin Cane, teaches me reversing and three-point turns on the disused bomber dispersals. For the test, the rig is full uniform – with wings. Surely with wings a chap ought to be able to drive? Also, with Cambridge so flat, there's nowhere to fail the hill start. The examiner gives the thumbs up and the Morris does a great job ferrying thirsty Pilot Officers around the pubs and trainee nurses of Cambridge.

All goes to plan until Boxing Day, when it starts to snow. The temperature hardly rises above freezing until Easter and the runway becomes snow-bound. An attempt to clear the stuff with the hot exhaust of Vampire jets results in ice 3 inches thick, which has to be chipped off by us aircrews with picks and shovels. It's hot and tiring work, relieved only by the twice-daily arrival of the NAAFI wagon bearing bacon butties and steaming mugs of tea. After a week, half the runway width is clear and we ferry the Varsities off to nearby RAF Wyton, where the course resumes, flying from a vast bomber runway.

But in January 1963, on the day of Sukarno's confrontational declaration – halfway through the intended course and after just forty-five hours' flying – three of us from Cranwell are ordered to report to 242 Operational Conversion Unit (OCU) at RAF Thorney Island on the south coast. Brian Nicolle, Mike Cross and myself have been posted for training on the new Argosy transport destined in a few short months we're told, to reinforce RAF air power in the Far East.

At that time, the British taxpayer was funding no fewer than three air bases on Singapore Island, together with a naval base and half-a-dozen garrisons – a strong hand with which to support the forces on the ground in Borneo. There were also two well-placed forward airbases.

Kuching, 400 miles from Singapore in the British colony of Sarawak, was the capital of the colonial Rajahs Brooke for two hundred years. RAF Kuching lodged on the civilian airfield. The area was under threat from Indonesian forces on the Kalimantan frontier – just 'five fighting days away' according to Major General Walker.

The island of Labuan, 800 miles north-east of Singapore, was the main Japanese air and naval base in the Second World War and had since been a regular staging post for the RAF, administered from Changi. Traffic and resources built up quickly here after the Brunei Rebellion.

RAF transport aircraft were detached to Borneo. From RAF Seletar, Beverleys and Twin Pioneers went to Labuan to fly missions in the hazardous mountainous uplands of north-eastern British Borneo. Valettas from RAF Butterworth in north-west Malaya were based in Kuching, to supply the forward jungle forts of no less challenging southern Sarawak. Here, they were joined in July 1963 by four-engined Hastings transports from RAF Changi.

The RAF also had the Shackleton maritime patrol aircraft at Changi, together with Far East Communications Flight and the Meteors of the Target Towing Flight. Seletar had the helicopter squadrons with the Sycamore, Whirlwind and twin-rotored Belvedere. Tengah was the fighter and bomber base: Hunters and Javelins to patrol the borders and escort the freighters, and the dual-role Canberra – photo-reconnaissance aircraft and bomber.

Indonesia had more. They had an arms deal with the Soviet Union that strengthened their armed forces in the successful 1962 struggle against the remaining Dutch province in West Irian Java. American Mustang fighters, Mitchell bombers and C-130 transports, as well as the Russian MiGs and Badgers, gave them potential superiority in the air.

In the late spring, Indonesian guerrillas began to move into Sarawak. Volunteers from the Clandestine Communist Organisation (CCO) were in support, subverting the local tribes. Villages and police stations were attacked and villagers kidnapped and killed. Early on Good Friday, a force of thirty bandits surrounded the police station at Tebedu in West Sarawak, shot dead a policeman and looted the bazaar.

In Britain, the government ordered the media to keep the Borneo story in low profile while diplomatic work continued behind the scenes. But out in the Far East, the involvement of British forces in further full-scale fighting was looking inevitable.

Three months after the Tebedu raid, an Argosy from 242 OCU is at 14,000 feet in the clear blue skies over southern France. It's one of a fleet that's spent a week in the heat and dust of RAF Idris near Tripoli. Because of opposition to night-flying from the Hayling Island Residents' Association – chaired by the retired General Horrocks – the whole OCU has at tax-payers' expense decamped to the southern Mediterranean, to practise night circuits and cross-country flights over the uninhabited desert sands.

Libya, with its King Idris, is a strategic ally of Great Britain. It's only six years since the Suez crisis and neighbouring Egypt is still a bit prickly. Monarchies are not much in fashion in the Middle East and the king needs all the friends he can get. The Yanks are there too, Wheelus USAF Base providing a turning point on the navigation exercise.

So from the air, we RAF transport crews can marvel at the ruined Roman cities of this ancient country – a battlefield not so very long ago. On the ground, we follow in the footsteps of the Desert Rats in bringing welcome foreign exchange to Tripoli and Tobruk – where at the La Bamba nightclub the star turn's a bottle-blonde stripper from Croydon. We relax in the station swimming pool and sip whisky-sours at the bar.

Some of us are dragooned into playing cricket against the Station team and survive temperatures never experienced at the Oval.

The Argosies refuelled at Orange in Southern France on the flight down to North Africa, but the return flight is to be direct, back to Thorney Island in time to get away for the weekend. Downstairs are two dozen aircrew travelling as passengers and behind me on the jump seat, perches an eagle-eyed Training Pilot. Even these exalted beings need to heed the call of nature and just twenty minutes south of Paris, he disappears downstairs.

That's the moment when one of the fire-warning lights on the pilots' Standard Warning System decides to illuminate.

These warning lights are notoriously fickle, often triggered by nothing more dangerous than static electricity. However, the trainee captain, Flight Lieutenant Bob Scott, is understandably cautious – on the last flight with his previous squadron he deposited his York transport 100 feet short of the runway at the Indian Ocean staging-post of Gan. He can picture it, still there, intact and splendid in 50 feet of water.

So it's into engine-fire drills.

With number four engine feathered and stopped and the first extinguisher fired, the light's still glowing on the instrument panel. Bob fires the second and final burst of foam. The fire-warning light stays on.

A ruffled Training Pilot arrives at speed at the top of the ladder, his precious moments of privacy cut short by the alarming change of engine note. But there's nothing even he can do. Hopes of an early weekend getaway fade. We can't continue to England on three engines and are obliged to make an emergency radio call and land at the nearest diversion airfield.

I transmit on the emergency frequency: 'PAN – PAN – PAN – position ten miles south of Paris – flight-level one-two-zero – one-seven-double-zero zulu time – one engine stopped – no further emergency – request diversion.'

Back comes the instruction: 'Divert to Le Bourget.' It's an airfield a few miles to the north of Paris.

That's what we do. The crew carries out the procedures immaculately and Bob makes a text-book three-engined approach and landing at Le Bourget. Right in the middle of the Paris Airshow.

The crowd's impressed and cheers enthusiastically. *Voilà – les Rosbifs sont formidables!* The crew rather enjoys it too and the Training Pilot's pleased with the performance. The aircrew passengers downstairs aren't so happy though. Here they are, with what looks like the gift of a night in Paris with chic French dollies for company and their only kit is what they stand up in – standard-issue British khaki-drill shirts and pantomime shorts.

But galloping to the rescue comes the co-pilot's flight imprest, the money entrusted to him for just such an emergency as this. The drinks are cheap and the shorts are declared *mignon*. By the time an aircraft arrives from Thorney Island with replacement extinguishers, there's a high old party on the go. Tommy Norcross, one of the navigators and fresh off the V-bomber force, is surrounded by entranced Air France lovelies. In dulcet Lancastrian tones he's crooning a seductive serenade: the tune is from *My Fair Lady*, but the words are all his own. 'All I want is my end away ....'

Both aeroplanes take off for base in the dark, their aircrews late for the weekend getaway but happy. On Monday morning, there's hell to pay with the Squadron Leader Admin over the imprest.

The night-flying episode was a highlight of No. 9 Argosy Course: four months of operational training – following a four-week aircraft factory course with Armstrong Whitworth at Baginton near Coventry, two weeks with Rolls-Royce at Derby for the engines and a week with Smiths in Gloucester for the avionics.

That time in the industrial centres of the Midlands and the North was an eye-opener for us fledgling co-pilots and our new chums the navigators, many of whom were first tour junior officers, too. Morris 8s and Austin 12s laboured up the perilous, brand-new M1 in the snow. We met the captains and flight engineers, to us very senior guys. One of the first-tour captains, Flight Lieutenant John 'Horse' Horsfall, made an immediate impression by winning a hundred quid on the dogs in Derby. When we got to know him better, he told us that he had spent most of his time in the sixth form playing semi-professional snooker in Wimbledon.

In Derby, I was in digs with Flying Officer Pat Gorman, another first-tour co-pilot and a good-looking guy. With an eye to the beer kitty we tried to persuade him to do a bit of male modelling on the side. We turned up at Mrs B's in time for tea and were met by a landlady all at sixes and sevens. She said she was very sorry but would we mind having our meal in the kitchen? Sadly, her dad had died and he and his coffin would be occupying the dining-room table until his funeral in the morning. Then, at the Officers' Mess at RAF Innsworth a lovely young airwoman brought in early-morning tea for a whole week. The lads trembled in their beds.

At RAF Thorney Island, two months were spent in the Ground School learning the operational procedures for the Argosy, and half listening to tedious meteorology lectures on Inter-Tropical Convergence Zones (ITCZ) and their storms and turbulence. We were introduced to the flight simulator – a state-of-the-art machine with hydraulic attitude mechanisms and video mock-up of the view through the windscreen. Some found it nonetheless disorientating, but the real thing was fine, with panoramic views of the Isle of Wight, the Solent and Chichester Harbour. Alongside the senior aircraft at the OCU – Hastings and Beverleys – the Argosy fleet was new and shiny.

Collins' dictionary defines an Argosy as a 'large, richly laden merchant-ship', which sounded pretty good to us. It was designed by Armstrong Whitworth to an Air Ministry specification for a medium-range transport, demanding at the same time that it be compliant with civilian airworthi-ness Performance Group A. This meant it could lose an engine at any stage of flight and still continue safely. The designers pinched bits and pieces of design from Hawker-Siddeley Aviation, the parent Group: the wing off the Avro Shackleton, the engines from the Vickers Viscount and the tail booms from the Gloster Meteor fuselage. This resulted in losses in airframe efficiency, and rate-of-climb, airspeed and payload all suffered. But the load versatility given by the clam-shell doors balanced the ledger, as did the state-of-the-art avionics (attitude and direction display system from Smiths) and navigation aids (in particular the Marconi AD2300 Doppler with a twin along/across track display). It was flying at the cusp of 1960s technology.

Down on the south coast, after the deep freeze of the winter, it was a golden summer. Brian Close was defying the West Indies fast bowlers up at Lord's. Beatles music was everywhere and the pubs and clubs were swinging – from the *Pomme d'Or* dive in Pompey to the pub in Bosham where, after a couple of pints, you could 'see France across the water'. It didn't matter that the water was Chichester Creek and France, the village of West Thorney.

Some days before the Libya trip, the aircrews are called to Sick Quarters to have their jabs: yellow fever, typhoid, tetanus, the lot. Since this cocktail usually immobilises the limb, the left arm generally gets the needle. In the evening, three of us set off for Portsmouth in the Morris 8. Pilot Officer Tom Sneddon, one of the first-tour navigators, is in the back and Flight Lieutenant Mick Bathe, a burly second-tour pilot, more than fills the passenger seat. I steer with my working right arm.

'On my command, Mick, you change gear.'

'Right-ho, Rog. Chocks away!'

All goes well as past the Guardroom we sail and onto the half-mile causeway leading to the mainland.

'Eyes left, guys!'

We're passing a gang of girls out for the evening, and the lads whistle loudly in appreciation and wave their good right arms. With broad smiles, the dolly-birds wave back, and when I call, 'Top gear, Mick!' his mind's not on the job. His beefy arm slams us into reverse – and at 25 miles-an-hour this is not helpful. Gearwheels shatter and the car grinds to a halt. Dreams of a night in Pompey fade. Slowly – and backwards, stuck in reverse – we drive again past the hooting girls, past the bemused guards – to spend the evening in the Officers' Mess, drinking a valedictory glass or six to the Morris's mangled gearbox.

The aircrews had known for some time that this preparation in Sussex was for posting to Singapore, to the re-formed 215 Squadron based at Changi to reinforce the freighting and supply-dropping force in Borneo. RAF archives informed us that 215 Squadron was originally No. 15 Squadron of the Royal Naval Air Service (RNAS), formed near Dunkirk in March 1918. It took its badge, with a gold-crowned porcupine, from the arms of Coudekerque, a village nearby. Its motto, *Surgite nox adest* (Arise, night is at hand) reflected the squadron's night bomber role at the time. It became a transport unit in 1945, with Dakotas in Singapore, and after nearly two decades a piece of history was to be repeated.

Possibly because of the recent Malayan Emergency and the subsequent noises coming out of Indonesia, it was thought that the Argosy would make an effective counter-insurgency platform. The boffins developed devices for hanging cameras and small bombs from the fuselage and a couple of crews were sent for bombing training. One aircraft was modified, but the trained crews prayed that these systems might never be used in anger. What if a bomb hung up? What if the insurgents shot back?

In July, we were qualified Argosy crews and promoted to the rank of Flying Officer. On two weeks' embarkation leave, blue serge uniforms went into storage, the Morris 8s and Austin 12s were sold and kitbags stuffed with standard-issue khaki tropical uniforms. Under cloudy August skies, we bade fond farewells to tearful girlfriends and bravely smiling parents. They had read the occasional press reports on Sukarno's plans for Indonesia and the proposed Malaysia and weren't at all sure about their loved-ones floating around out there in unarmed cargo planes.

But for us it was a gripping prospect. Changi was the Shangri-La of RAF postings, with all the mystery of the Orient. And we were going into action. Climbing into the Comet 2 at RAF Lyneham in Wiltshire, the talk was of jungles, mountains and MiGs.

CHAPTER THREE

Action Stations

On 19 August 1963 the dapper figure of the Officer Commanding 215 Squadron, Wing Commander Tony Talbot-Williams, waited on the tarmac at Paya Lebar (Singapore's international airport) for the Comet 2 of RAF Transport Command to taxi onto its allocated slot. There was a sharp crease down the sleeves of his khaki uniform bush-jacket and his shoes were shiny. Squaring his shoulders, he prepared to greet the latest and last batch of aircrew, bringing his newly re-formed squadron up to full strength.

The twenty-four hour flight from Lyneham had included refuelling stops at the bases of El Adem in Libya, Aden, in southern Arabia and Gan in the Indian Ocean, each a reminder of a vanishing British Empire. The buildings alongside the desert and island airstrips were mostly corrugated iron Twyneham huts, and at Gan RAF personnel on thirteen-month postings had gone weak at the knees at the sight of the women passengers' trendy mini-skirts.

Day or night, stepping out of the aircraft's air-conditioning was like walking into a steam bath. Clothes that had seemed cool and neat in Wiltshire were now wet blankets, and sweating hands and faces made every cigarette a sponge. On the last leg, the toddlers on board became really fractious and one little girl failed to hold down her dinner. Horse, her unfortunate dad, was forced to borrow a pair of shorts from me. Much too long, they flapped damply round his knees.

Dishevelled, travel-stained and jet-lagged, the eagerly awaited reinforcements straggled down the steps, to be greeted by the wry smile of their Wing Commander.

The families are driven off to transit hotels and half-a-dozen of us bachelors, Mike, Brian, Pat and myself, Tom Sneddon and another first-tour navigator, Pilot Officer Geoff Walker are bussed to Temple Hill Officers' Mess, RAF Changi. Temple Hill is one of the more pleasant spots on Singapore Island, often blessed with a breeze off the sea half-a-mile to the north-east. Built in 1930 as the Artillery Officers' Mess, the white stucco building has colonial-style pillars and verandahs, anterooms with rattan cane armchairs and a billiard table and bar. This all looks good to us. We are given rooms on the top floor – three sharing and no air-conditioning, but with fans rotating on the ceiling to stir the humid heat.

We're too late for dinner but the bar's still open and, not for the last time, we fall among thieves – the old Changi-hands who introduce us innocents to the local Tiger beer. It comes on draught, a golden, ice cool and seemingly harmless lager – until the third, fourth or fifth pint. You need it to quench the thirst, but the thirst seems unquenchable.

Some of those inspecting us new arrivals – including five from 215 Squadron who flew in a month ago – take us under their wing, suggesting we go and eat at somewhere called Bedok Corner. We climb into a fleet of four ancient taxis and bucket out of camp, past Changi Gaol, its grim outline stark in the moonlight, and down along the coast road. The heady smell of Singapore hits our nostrils, a pungent mixture of sea, seaweed and sewage. We are hot, sticky, tiddly and hungry.

We pull up at a terrace of ramshackle stalls by the seashore, just where the road turns sharply towards Singapore town. They're garishly lit by naked kerosene flares. Their light shows a squad of white-shirted Chinamen, stirring and tossing all manner of aromatic food in woks over hissing gas flames: prawns, squid, crab and clams, pork and chicken, Chinese vegetables, rice boiled or fried and several sorts of noodle.

We meet Mr Lim, who is introduced as the old hands' favourite among the Chinese cooks. We order the equivalent of the dish-of-the-day and within minutes are dining like colonial rajahs. The food is a revelation and belies the unsavoury look of the stalls. It's fresh and delicious – washed down with more Tiger beer, this time in bottles, sunk into buckets of iced water. It all costs just a few Singapore dollars – about half-a-crown each. On our first night we've been initiated into the most popular of Changi pastimes – dining out at Mr Lim's.

Back in our cavernous room at the Mess, we sleep deeply despite the heat and racket of the tropical night – frogs, cicadas and clicking house lizards. The next morning, there are no ill effects from the food and only one or two from the beer. We don our pantomime shorts, take a light breakfast in the elegant surroundings of the Mess and are soon rolling down the hill in the squadron bus to report for duty.

In the front seat is one of the guys from last night, a young but confident navigator, Flying Officer 'Art' Smith, more than ready to point out the sights. The route takes us through the outskirts of the Far East Air Force (FEAF) headquarters on the hills up to Fairy Point, where the

HQ Officers' Mess commands a splendid view of the sea on three sides. The bus passes Changi Hospital, half-a-dozen three-storey white concrete buildings sitting up in the healthiest air on the Island. Nearby is the Hospital Mess.

'In there, live twenty-two nursing sisters,' says our volunteer guide, with a gleam in his eye.

Down the hill, along a shady avenue of teak trees and past the colonial buildings of Station Headquarters – the Changi Spitfire standing proudly alongside – we roll into Changi Village with its bustling, mostly open-fronted shops.

'Jong Sing over there,' he points out one of the few with a plate-glass window, 'is the best tailor – and he's got air-conditioning. He'll kit you out in the local-style khaki drill. Did me the full set.' He counts out on his fingers, 'Three pairs of shorts, one of longs, three shirts, three pairs of long socks, one bush-jacket, one sharkskin mess jacket. And he threw in some civvie shorts and slacks – all for a hundred and fifty dollars – less than seventeen quid.'

'Blimey, how long did that lot take?'

'Well, believe it or not, just twenty-four hours.'

The bus passes the Changi Creek Transit Hotel, a corrugated iron affair where, Art says, the crews have their pre-dawn breakfast before route flights. The airfield perimeter road along Changi beach is lined with palms and casuarinas.

'The Kiwis live over there; 41 Squadron RNZAF. See their Bristol Freighters? Bloody slow old crates – fly all over the Far East at 150 miles-an-hour. And next door's 205 Squadron. Their Shacks can do twelve or fourteen hours at a stretch at zero feet on sea patrols.'

Almost on the beach, in the scrub and behind a barbed-wire fence, is a collection of timber huts with what look like palm-thatched roofs. Art waves his arm in their direction.

'Those *bashas* belong to the FEAF Jungle Survival School.' He pulls a face in mock horror. 'We'll be down there before long – ten days in the bloody *bundu* with the creepy-crawlies. All right if you like that kind of thing.'

Our base of operations, the HQ of 215 Squadron, is a new concrete building standing just inside the perimeter fence, and painted a surprising shade of turquoise. Eight Argosies are proudly ranged on the tarmac dispersal.

'That used to be one of the runways,' says Art. 'Built by the prisoners in the war. They fixed it so that it was across the wind – pointing into the hills. Fouled things up for the Nips good and proper.' We believe him.

Thanking Art for the guided tour, we climb out of the bus and report to the Ops Room for induction to the squadron.

On a Saturday four weeks later, the squadron transport collects five of us bachelors at 1230 right outside our new home on Temple Hill, a *basha* again, but this time mainly of concrete. Already on the bus are the married captains and navigators, collected from their transit hotels, hirings and quarters around Changi and its neighbouring villages. Some are possibly not best pleased at leaving their families at the weekend – but not entirely unhappy at being called to action so early in the life of the squadron. It was only in July that the advance party of one captain and crew set up a temporary HQ in the 48 Squadron building at Changi, and a mere three weeks later that the aircraft and crews arrived after a four-day ferry flight from RAF Benson, their base in Oxfordshire.

Three days ago, on Sunday 15 September, the Federation of Malaysia was proclaimed and the event was celebrated by an air display at Paya Lebar. Three Argosies flew past in close formation and the FEAF band played in great style. The new state came into existence at midnight with Sarawak and North Borneo (renamed Sabah) forming the Eastern Division, and Malaya and Singapore, the Western. The next day, diplomatic relations were broken off all round – Indonesia with Malaysia, and Malaysia with Indonesia and the Philippines. A state of undeclared war existed. Encouraged by their leaders, thousands of Indonesian demonstrators (including most of the student population) stormed the British and Malaysian Embassies in the Indonesian capital, Djakarta, and at the same time their consulates in North Sumatra were sacked.

Yesterday afternoon and evening, angry mobs of Indonesians – men, youths and girls – attacked and burned the British Embassy and wrecked and looted the homes of British subjects. Screaming, 'Kill the British!' and 'Crush Malaysia!' they showed they meant business by digging up the cricket pitch.

With life and limb, and property, of British nationals in jeopardy, the Ambassador decided that evacuation would be the best course of action. A signal to Singapore placed the Changi transport crews on alert and today sees us abandoning our weekend plans in order to fly to Djakarta to the rescue.

'Things down there are not improving,' declares the Intelligence Officer. 'The British Military Attaché – a certain Major Muir Walker of the Black Watch – has been parading up and down in front of the Embassy, playing his bagpipes at full volume. The mob has not been impressed.'

After negotiations with the Indonesian authorities, safe passage has been promised and permission granted for the evacuation. Our three

Argosies are to be joined by a Hastings of 48 Squadron. We can overfly Sumatra and Java for the 600-mile trip to Djakarta, but we'll have to keep to specified airways. The flight time for the trip is estimated at three hours. There'll be no refuelling at the destination, so our tanks will be filled to the brim to get there and back. From the intelligence reports we note the position of the MiG fighter bases in Sumatra and the gun positions around Djakarta.

The radio log for this flight is vital. Communication with air traffic control needs to be prompt and clear or the Indonesian forces might very well become trigger-happy. On this international trip an FEAF call-sign is required, and our crew is to have the heroic-sounding 'Mike Oscar Kilo Oscar Golf'. Using it on the long-range high frequency radios – specially installed last night by the electricians – is going to be a new game.

In the locker-room we change into tropical flying suits and gather equipment, including Chinese oiled-paper umbrellas – a vital item of Far East kit. It's not raining now, but visibility is poor – down to half-a-mile because of smoke from Indonesian forest fires.

The aircraft dispersal is right alongside the squadron buildings, with the Argosies lined up in echelon formation. To help them get around their torrid workplace, the groundcrew have a fleet of Chinese trishaws. There's a prop change going on just now and two aircraftmen fitters are pedalling along, sweating under the weight of the 7 ft torque wrench needed for the job. Teams of contract Chinese manning the fuel bowsers complete the oriental scene.

The Squadron Commander captains the lead aircraft and I'm in the third on my allocated crew, with Boss Leary the captain and Rev Wilkins the navigator. XR448 is in passenger-rig, with twelve rows of blue leatherette seats, rearward-facing and four-abreast. The flight engineer, Mister Howarth, and the AQM, Sergeant Bateman, are as usual checking everything out.

Take-offs are to be staggered at ten-minute intervals for safety separation. Our engines scream into life and XR448 taxies out. The single north/south runway, already a mile and-a-half long, is being extended to take the heavier jet transports coming into service, and the taxiways are restricted by the building works. Extra care is needed. The other day an Argosy turned into a dead-end and, with no reverse-pitch props – unlike the Beverley that can lurch majestically astern with all the grace of an elephant – its passengers had to get out and push the aircraft back to try again.

With a full fuel load, the Argosy powers into the air. On the starboard side we can see into the infamous exercise yard of Changi Gaol, still in use and a sobering sight.

The skipper turns to port and sets a course for Sumatra. Straight away we're over the Indonesian islands just across the Singapore Straits and we must make contact with their Air Traffic Control. I'm relieved to hear them come up loud and clear – and speaking the Queen's English too, the *lingua franca* of the air.

The visibility improves as we gain height and for a good half-hour our route parallels the coast. Just 100 miles south of Singapore, we pass over Lingga Island, marking the Equator. Crossing it is a first for me, but it's not the time for celebrations. From here we run across Sumatra and thunderstorms are looming up ahead. Within minutes, the Argosy plunges into them.

We're at 8,000 feet and the anvil-headed clouds tower miles above us – we can't get over them. There's a line of them across our track and we can't go round them – we have to stay on the airway. So we plough through them. At this height the wind shears are at their most violent. Rain smashes against the windscreen and lightning crackles and flashes along the conductor-wires above the booms. The autopilot's thrown out and the turboprops wail as the aircraft tosses and turns. It's all a tremendous racket. I sit white-faced and queasy and sweat it out.

At least we know where we are. On Indonesian independence, the Dutch firm Philips left behind one of the best telecommunications networks in the world. The navigator's got us locked onto the beacons along the airway and the Doppler continues to plot track and distance. We report to Air Traffic Control over Palembang beacon – just over halfway now.

We nurse the aircraft down to the southern tip of Sumatra and across the narrow straits to Java. The weather's clearer down here and bits of the terrain can be picked out. It looks much like Borneo but more cultivated. Are those pepper plantations? That must be Djakarta, just 30 miles ahead on the northern coast. Air Traffic Control gives us permission to make a radio beacon approach.

But for once, the navigator's confused. There are two radio beacons at Djakarta and he's uncertain which one to follow. The one chosen throws us some miles off course and we miss our approach and have to go round again – not the most relaxing exercise in the circumstances. The hair rises on my neck at the thought of Indonesian anti-aircraft guns below.

Mercifully, no MiG fighter is scrambled to intercept, and no tracer rushes up to meet us. Air Traffic Control makes no comment as the Argosy finally swoops in to land, stirring up clouds of spray – the rain is pouring down again.

The ground controller sends us several hundred yards from the airport terminal, to join the other Argosies, safely arrived, at a distant dispersal area close to the seashore and up against the barbed wire of the perimeter fence. The Hastings lands soon after and we prepare ourselves to wait – surrounded by armed Indonesian soldiers. Sergeant Bateman joins us on the flight deck with a tray of tea and biscuits, and peers through the windscreen.

'Notice anything funny, Skip?'

'What – with the Indos?'

'Yep, that's right. Guns are pointing the wrong way. Aren't they meant to be holding off the hostile natives?'

After a nervous ninety minutes, dusk falls. Then, out of the gloom, a column of men, women and children appear – nearly two hundred of them, straggling along the perimeter road outside the wire. In the lead is the unlikely, but unmistakable, figure of the famous Major Walker in full highland rig, still playing the bagpipes with gusto. The staff and families from the British Embassy are marching in the pouring rain away from the mayhem in Djakarta, into the care of the RAF.

It's a moving sight. The wet and bedraggled British refugees carry what possessions they can – suitcases, roughly tied bundles, even the odd bit of furniture. Babies are crying and brothers and sisters cling to their mums, hugging precious toys. There are tears of relief at seeing us and our aircraft with their familiar RAF roundels, as the Indonesian soldiers chivvy them through a gate in the wire. Encumbered by their assorted baggage, they clamber up the wet steps into the aircraft cabins. There are more people than we have seats for, so we settle them down in the cabins as comfortably as we can and move among them with hot tea.

One little boy asks where his daddy is and after a headcount, several of the Embassy staff appear to be missing. But there's no time to wait. The Indonesian troops are getting increasingly restless and the flight-plan permissions are close to running out. A long-distance transmission to Changi using the powerful new radio arranges a mopping-up flight for the following day.

One by one, the aircraft taxi away from the glowering soldiers. Roaring down the runway, they climb into the pitch darkness and plough their way homewards through the storms. The evacuees start to dry out and are restored with soup and rolls by the AQMs. The aircraft gangways are crowded with children playing on the floor, until, exhausted, they fall asleep where they are. The adults compare stories of the hardship and dangers of the past days and try to prepare for the uncertain time to come.

Two-and-a-half hours later the fleet lands back at Changi, to be welcomed by the assembled diplomatic staff, military intelligence and the world's media. Some 400 people are evacuated in all and Indonesia is cleared of the British and their friends. There's to be no further over-flying of Indonesian territory by the RAF for many months.

On the day after the evacuation, Britain informs the Malaysian Prime Minister, Tunku Abdul Rahman, that under the terms of the Mutual Assistance Treaty, she is ready to assist in defending Malaysia's independence. The offer is accepted and the build up of British forces gathers pace. Let battle commence.

Long Jawi is a Sarawak village right up in the headwaters of the Rajang, the longest river in Borneo. It lies in a steep wooded valley under the 5,000-feet summit of Batu Kayo in the spinal range, just 40 miles from Indonesian Kalimantan. The country either side of the border is wild and inhospitable, inhabited in 1963 only by nomadic tribes of Punans – blowpipe-hunters and gatherers.

Ten days after the Djakarta evacuation, a force of 150 Indonesian guerrillas came down this valley wielding their *parangs,* to launch a surprise attack on the village in the first determined military raid of Confrontation. The defenders – six men of the 1st/2nd Goorkha Rifles, two Police Field Force signallers and twenty-one Iban Border Scouts – fought bravely but were overwhelmed.

The raiders looted the village and set the police station on fire. Five of the defenders were killed, including the two signallers. Trekking for four days through the jungle, the survivors brought word back to base. The counter-attack was immediate. Helicopters carried Gurkha soldiers to cut off the valleys above Long Jawi and the retreating Indonesians took heavy casualties.

British commanders learnt from this attack that winning the hearts and minds of tribesmen was going to be vital. The Indonesians had infiltrated Long Jawi two days before the raid, but not one native had dared tell the Gurkhas. The immediate and effective response showed the Ibans that the British meant business. Rustling up at will helicopter-loads of fierce Gurkhas (terrifying with their curved-bladed *kukri*) and Scotsmen (equally fearsome with their self-loading rifles) was to be an important factor in the campaign. Equally important was maintaining patrols on the border, among the tribes, and keeping soldiers out in the jungle for weeks rather than days by supporting them from the air.

The transport squadrons of Singapore started to fly a shuttle service to the Labuan base, a trip of some three-and-a-half hours, and to Kuching in Sarawak, an hour less. An almost constant stream of Hastings, Argosies and New Zealand Bristol Freighters from Changi, and Beverleys from Seletar carried thousands of tons of supplies and equipment and battalions of troops, at all times of the day and night.

Logistics staff performed miracles of personnel movement and freight loading. On occasion, it was more than miraculous. At least two Beverleys were double-loaded with ammunition boxes, but managed to stagger 600-odd miles across the South China Sea.

Bulk and heavy freight went by sea to Kuching and Labuan. Some supplies could be transported by longboat up the mighty rivers of the Borneo lowlands – there were few passable roads in Borneo. However, soldiers of the RASC broke the majority down into loads for air-freighting or airdrop.

Supplies and men were landed in Twin Pioneers at forward airstrips extended by the Royal Engineers and the RAF Airfield Construction Branch, assisted by the troops themselves. These strips quickly became familiar to the airdrop crews as the DZs where aviation fuel and other bulk supplies were dropped.

Much of this freight was then further broken down for carrying forward to the jungle patrols, sometimes by canoe, but mostly by helicopter. The bravery of the helicopter crews of the RAF and the Royal Navy, became the stuff of legend. Carrying out a crippling workload in terrible weather and almost impossible terrain, they were vital in maintaining close support of the four-man SAS patrols operating on the 700-mile border, each covering some 10,000 yards of mountainous jungle frontier.

These patrols, increasingly reinforced with Gurkhas and Paras, operated close to the tribes, gaining their trust and loyalty, and gathering information about the Indonesian troops and their native collaborators, willing or otherwise. They kept their equipment to a minimum, relying on the weekly air-supply for food, clothing and ammunition. In this way British forces, although massively outnumbered, were able to dominate the Indonesians, regulars and irregulars alike.

The first 215 Squadron Argosy detachment in Labuan starts on 29 October, called to support the Beverleys. More fuel is needed at the forward helicopter bases than even these stalwarts can carry.

Ours, the first crew, flies missions for seven days in a row. We go back again to Long Semado and Ba Kelalan, and twice more to the heavenly Bario. We make four afternoon sorties, but only once do we fail to make the drop. Lio Matu, Long Banga and Long Akah – all in the highlands – are notable both for their dramatic terrain and restricted dropping areas. At all three we put one into the river.

We make two 1-ton drops at Belaga – a three-hour round trip and one that we make twice in one long day. It's not easy to find down south in deepest Sarawak, and bucketing along in the afternoon with a full load and the storms at their worst, is an endurance test for crew and aircraft.

When, after a twelve-hour day we get back to the Airport Hotel bar, we're ready for our Tiger beer. We meet the other aircrews, including the Twin Pioneer and helicopter pilots. We listen to their stories of nights in longhouses, living the life of gods from on high with dancing, rice wine and women. But it's not all roses. One of the helicopter guys lost a mate a week before when his machine crashed through the 300-feet trees. They've not found it yet – most likely they never will.

One night, we hear about the airborne assault on Bario, the first action out of Labuan in the Confrontation campaign proper. Four Twin Pioneers airlifted fifty Greenjackets, with three Whirlwind helicopters flying in close support, and a Beverley and three Valettas resupplying bullets and howitzer shells.

The very next day we're tasked to go again to Belaga, supporting a similar assault with two consecutive loads of eight 1-ton containers. This time there are thirty-two Indonesian fatalities. We're strangely detached at 700 feet above the action – and then it's back to the bar afterwards. But we get much closer to the firing line than we'd like on our next foray, into Sabah, where the terrain is even wilder and largely unexplored.

We take a delivery of eight 1-ton containers to Sepulot, a jungle strip slap-bang in the middle of the unmapped part and at the bottom of the very steep and high-sided Talankai valley. We reckon that's bad enough, but then we go to Pensiangan.

At some 2,000 feet in the Sabah highlands, we find this village and infantry fort no more than a dozen miles from the border where two rivers meet, and ringed with hills up to 4,000 feet high. The Intelligence Officer briefs us on what we might expect.

'The Sambakung river flows down over the border from Pensiangan and for the Indos it's a regular highway in their attempts to outflank us and attack from the rear. It's a hot-bed of small-arms fire. But from the air you won't be able to tell they're shooting at you – until you get hit.'

Just the expectation adds an edge.

Boss Leary hasn't done a recce on this one – a Beverley might be able to get in, but it certainly couldn't get out again. We can just get in from the top end of the valley but can't level out in time to drop the load, and from the bottom end we can drop, but the climb-out is impossible. The skipper therefore works out a figure-of-eight pattern in the valleys, at 1,000 feet below the hilltops and ridges, and that brings us in across the main river. It's only manageable in good weather and is virtually blind – but a prominent dead tree gives just the right line. When the red light comes on, the DZ – the village green – is invisible. It comes into view at the last moment and it's, 'Green on!' straight away. As the load goes out, it's a heart-stopping, full emergency-power climb – lose an engine and we're

done for. With a racking left turn to clear the ridge beyond, we make it –
and repeat the pattern many times. At the end of the mission, the groundcrew have to clear the lower aerials of branches and leaves.

At the debriefing the Intelligence guy has a signal in his hand.

'It says here that during your drop firing was heard by the patrols at the
DZ. Actually, chaps, it's quite difficult to hit an aircraft from the ground
with a general purpose machine-gun.'

That cheers us up. A little.

But it's not the Indonesian small-arms fire that's the biggest hazard –
it's the mountainous terrain. And the weather. We spend many an hour
circling over the valleys waiting for the mist to burn away. Often it
doesn't, and the only option is to spiral down through a gap in cloud to
get to the DZ. Flying blind is a test of a pilot's nerve at any time, but one
that's unparalleled up in these Borneo highlands.

Then another crew from the squadron flies out to relieve us. Before
I leave for Changi their co-pilot asks what it's been like. He gives the
impression he'd far rather be at home with his family on a Sunday night,
so I play down the bullets and bumps a bit, and tell him he'll be glad he
came – the scenery's phenomenal and this supply-dropping lark's a piece
of cake. As the Tiger beer flows I almost begin to believe it myself. But I lie
in my camp bed that night, mosquitoes buzzing round my ears, and hear
again the Argosy's wailing engines. I see a wall of towering trees and in
alcohol-induced sleep, dream of Pensiangan.

No. 215 Squadron continued its first Labuan supply-dropping detachment for another three weeks, each outgoing crew flying with the in-
coming team on its first mission to show them the ropes.

The captains were a mixed bag of pilots. Some grand old transport
hands rather looked down on tactical support flying and others from
flying training wanted to do everything exactly by the book. The half-
dozen first tour captains sported a devil-may-care attitude but it was the
ex-Beverley men who really relished operating at the limits at low altitude,
and at first, did it best.

The navigators started to draw maps of the various DZs and annotate
navigation charts with the few identifiable features, handing them on to
the next crew. Hearing the reports of small-arms fire, more than one took
to wearing a flak jacket when prone in the supply-aiming position in the
nose – with another around the nether regions for extra comfort and
security.

As well as the 1-ton containers and double bags on the airstrips, the
Argosies began dropping in close support too, delivering 100-lb harness
packs, also known as SEAC packs since their introduction to South East

Asia Command in Burma and Malaya in the Second World War. They were manhandled through the side doors and dropped on a single parachute into smaller DZs. These were sometimes existing clearings, perhaps on a riverbank, a cultivated plot or a volleyball court near a village, but frequently they were no more than 20 square-yards hacked out of the jungle for the purpose by a patrol. Often they were blasted out with explosives. Marked sometimes by a 2-feet diameter orange balloon floating clear of the 200-feet trees or by coloured smoke, these were the greatest challenge for the aircrew.

'Like dropping a flippin' duster from an upstairs window into a dustbin, in a high wind,' as one frustrated navigator put it. 'Aerial darts,' said another. The air-release height for these packs was just 500 feet, which in the steep mountain valleys made for interesting flying.

On his first solo detail, Tom Sneddon had to find three of these challenging DZs. The map references were given by the patrols themselves, and they didn't necessarily know where they were. The crew spent a dicey forty-five minutes looking for the first, a drop to the Royal Leicesters. The next was easier to find. When they got to the third, they reckoned it was over the border – and it turned out it was. After a nervous drop they beat a hasty retreat and got back to base after a sortie of three-and-a-quarter hours – to set off for another in the afternoon.

After a day like that the bar offered essential relief. Tiger beer was a great restorative – it also loosened tongues. One evening a 2nd Lieutenant of the Royal Leicesters buttonholed the Argosy crew to complain.

'Pretty feeble effort the other day up at Long Pasia, wasn't it?'

'What the hell d'you mean, chum?' Steve Stephens, the captain, was a forthright kind of guy.

'Sprayed the whole bally delivery all over the *bundu*, didn't you? Can't be that hard to get those things on the bullseye?'

Steve fixed him with a steely look. 'Perhaps you'd like to come along and see for yourself. Free tomorrow?'

He was, and they took him on a drop at Pensiangan, where eight 1-ton containers of petrol all hit the DZ. The 2nd Lieutenant came back wiser and greyer and in urgent need of a change of underwear.

The Argosies began to feel the strain. The rear clam-shell doors were working beyond their design limits. Occasionally, 'chutes failed to release from the bag, badly jerking the anchor cable and straining the hydraulic jacks and door hinges. On one mission the doors failed to lock open and on another there was damage to the jack and they wouldn't close. There were equipment fires and smoke fumes, and fin fairings damaged by the parachute static lines. But overall, the airframe performed manfully and the turboprops were magnificently reliable. With their hugely complicated piston engines, the Beverley crews suffered problems every fourth take-off, but in contrast, the rate for the Argosy's Darts was statistically insignificant. The crews gave thanks for Messrs Rolls and Royce.

When the first Argosy detachment at Labuan finished on 22 November, only a couple of sorties had been abandoned – because of impossible weather.

The Station Commander, Wing Commander Thomas AFC was moved to say: 'I am very appreciative of the contribution the Argosy has made and the excellent results achieved so early in the squadron's life. I shall call upon them again at reasonably short notice if operations demand.'

They did, and he did. Often.

CHAPTER FOUR

Work and Play

Back at Changi, life was scarcely less hectic. The steady 80-degree temperatures and clammy air took a bit of getting used to. In the heat, the Chinese tailor's shorts were liberating. They were smart too, as long as they conformed to regulation length. Horse persuaded John Hare that it would be stylish to have them slightly shorter, with the result that they couldn't be seen below his uniform bush-jacket. He was invited by the Station Commander to leave the parade ground, since to any observers it appeared he had no trousers on.

Even this cotton and terylene drill was limp by mid-morning. But we enjoyed the services of a Chinese batman who collected our discarded clothes from the floor first thing and had them back, magically crisp and pressed, by lunchtime. After a shower and a new set of duds we were ready for action again in the afternoon.

There was plenty of flying. Co-pilot Monthly Continuation Training gave the captains an opportunity to give us tyros an hour or so of circuits and bumps, occasionally at night, with practice instrument and emergency approaches. One Saturday lunchtime I'm called unexpectedly from the Mess to fill an hour's slot, and find that it's a flying proficiency (Category) test to boot. I've had a couple in the bar but I don't let on. Gerry Garforth, the Training Pilot, has his suspicions and throws the works at me. Nine landings later, we finish up with a three-engined radar-guided approach, and 500 feet from landing he throttles back a second engine. I just manage to land the Argosy in one piece. It's been nearly two hours and I'm sweating like the proverbial pig, but sober again, and glad to get away with a C-cat.

We co-pilots were regularly sent up for an hour or two together for local practice, one in the left-hand and one in the right-hand seat, without a baby-sitting captain. This was great for our self-esteem (in charge of one of Her Majesty's aircraft, against the historic backdrop of Singapore), but it must often have been nerve-wracking for the engineer and navigator. The co-pilots were a varied bunch: eight on their first full tour – the three of us from Cranwell and Oakington and the others on Short-Service Commissions – and of the rest, three on their second tour, and three more on their third. These more senior guys were impatient for captaincy and not always easy to fly with – perhaps they wanted to prove a point to us College types.

Night-flying was a really sweaty affair. The aircraft had often been standing out in the sun all day and the flight deck was at an almost intolerable 140 degrees Fahrenheit. After an hour of this it was back to the bar at Temple Hill. However, flying suits were banned in the Mess, where dress rules were strict. After 7 o'clock, long trousers, collar and tie were required for the gents, and for the ladies, dresses – with petticoats. Our saving grace was a balustrade separating the open end of the bar from a four-foot-deep monsoon drain. The idea was to edge along its base, technically outside the bar but with access to the beer inside – providing our mates played ball. An eye on the drain behind us, we hung on with one hand, and with the other thankfully received the cold, brimming glasses of Tiger. When other squadrons were night-flying it got a bit crowded.

There were a lot of people at Changi, with over 1,500 serving men and women of all ranks, many of them with families. In addition, for every three on the military strength there were four civilians. There was a native village on the station, and countless local and expatriate support staff: nurses, met officers, Mess and catering managers, and teachers for the primary, secondary and grammar schools.

We bachelors had very little contact with the schools but quite a lot with the lady teachers. Half-a-dozen of them lived in their own *basha* hut at Temple Hill, together with the same number of WRAF officers and nursing sisters. Their presence around the place – a waft of scent, the swish of a skirt – brought colour to our male lives. They offered sisterly friendship and romantic possibilities.

There were half-a-dozen of these *bashas* lining the tarmac road circling the Mess. Each had concrete walls but slatted wooden windows to circulate what little draught there was. Along the length of the hut was a wooden-tiled roof and a verandah – a favourite noisy meeting and mating place for monkeys. The often-torrential rain cascaded into foot-wide monsoon drains – popular with snakes. On either side of a bath-house unit were six rooms, house and home for the duration. They were comfortable enough, furnished with a bed, wardrobe and chest of drawers, and the essential ceiling fan. I set up a tropical fish tank, without the bother of electric immersion heating, and stocked it with silver angels, russet Siamese fighters and rainbow guppies.

Half-a-mile from Temple Hill, by the sea, the Officers' Club was a great draw, with its café-restaurant, bar, barber, dance-floor and swimming pool. On Tuesday evenings, films were screened outdoors by the pool, one of them the latest hit, *South Pacific*. The on-screen action romanticised South East Asian military service and we lapped it up – so did the native children and their parents, happily watching the movie from behind the flimsy screen.

In September, the aircrew of 215 Squadron gave a cocktail party in XP444, a grounded Argosy, known as the 'Christmas Tree' as it had donated so many of its parts as spares. The officers of HQ FEAF and RAF Changi were invited, as were the squadron groundcrew a couple of hours later. To support the flying workload, these stalwarts had taken responsibility for first-line servicing and worked three six-hour shifts out in the heat and rain seven days a week. We thanked our lucky stars for them.

Every Wednesday night in Changi Village there was an Amahs' Market where all kinds of stuff could be bought pretty cheaply. The warm night air was full of the sounds of haggling and the smell of fish and chips specially fried for the occasion. Our modest service pay was withdrawn from the Changi branch of the Chartered Bank and distributed among the beaming shopkeepers. In exchange, they offered us real bargains: the made-to-measure outfits, genuine Omega watches, Selangor pewter tankards, radios, shoes and leather goods. But for leather bindings for flying logbooks, the specialists were the inmates of Changi Gaol.

There was plenty of sport on the menu if you wanted it: swimming, water polo, cross-country, basketball, golf, hockey, cricket, soccer, badminton, go-karting, netball, squash, tennis and table-tennis, volleyball, sailing, sub-aqua – and rugby. Two of the first-tour 215 Squadron navigators, Geoff Walker and Robbie Cooper, made it to the Combined Services XV and famously beat Selangor state by 5 points to 3 in the rain and mud of Kuala Lumpur. For the less athletic, there was a darts league at the Chalet Club on Wednesday and Friday nights, in which officers' teams were invited to compete. The Chalet was one of a score of clubs at Changi, catering for most interests, from angling to zoology. It was a social mecca for non-commissioned ranks, their families and friends, with the best parties and the lowest beer prices. Variety acts were a regular draw - they didn't get the Beatles but they did get Matt Monro. Competition to get into the Temple Hill darts team and into the Chalet was intense

We were aware of the weather, indoors and out, all the time. The worst storms were the 'Sumatras', like the ones we met on the way to Djakarta. In October we suffered them for twenty-five days in a row. Their 40-knot winds blew torrential rain – as much as 4 inches in a morning – through the slats of the *bashas*, under the porticos of the Mess and into the woks of

Mr Lim. Flying in them was almost impossible and sport was downright dangerous. Lightning killed a footballer on the pitch one afternoon and the same storm knocked over a Junior Technician on the Argosy dispersal. This was Charlie Peace, who turned out to have a metal plate in his head and metal pins in his legs. He was a virtual lightning conductor. He was also famously the father of thirteen children – all doubtless grateful for the life-saving skills of his colleague, Junior Technician Stafford, as was the CO who awarded him a Commendation.

The north-east monsoon brought more torrents – for twenty-eight days in November. In the December surge, nearly 14 inches fell – four in just one afternoon. By contrast our first two months had been relatively rainless with less than 3 inches – what there was disappeared down the monsoon drains and water was rationed. We had to shower when we could and hope we could soap and shampoo before it was cut off.

Station security measures became increasingly apparent. The threat of Indonesian sabotage led to the mounting of extra guards and the arming of the Station Police. Security fences went up and anti-aircraft guns appeared in sandbagged emplacements. But as yet, there was no curfew or movement restriction, so one Saturday we set out to explore off-base.

I've acquired the car of my dreams – a black fabric-roofed, four-cylinder 1.5-litre Riley saloon. It may not be new but it seems to go great guns. Three of us, Pat, Mike and myself, have teamed up with three of the girls, two WRAF Pilot Officers and a teacher, and we all pile into my pride and joy. It's a tight fit as we cruise down the East Coast Road, past Bedok Corner and along the palm-fringed shore towards Singapore City, about 6 miles from Changi. The old car has the luxury of a windscreen that can be wound open, letting in some air, and the front doors are hinged at the centre-post so we open them a crack as well.

We're told that brief shorts and revealing necklines are not appreciated, so we're properly dressed, the men in slacks and long-sleeved shirts, and the girls in modest frocks. But we look pretty drab alongside the locals. Malay men wear the sarong and round black cap and the women the *kebaya*, a close-fitting jacket of many colours. Indian women dress in the *sari*, and Sikhs in turbans and *dhoti* are a common sight. Many of the Chinese women sport multi-coloured figure-hugging, slit-to-the-thigh *cheongsams*.

There's a lot of traffic, but at least they drive on the left. We roll past the palm trees of the East Coast Road at a cautious 40 miles-per-hour. I watch out for swaying coolies with their cumbersome wicker baskets on poles across the shoulders, and children, chickens and goats roaming freely.

We drive by Kallang Park, not so long ago the main civilian airport.

'Know why it closed?' comes a voice from the back. 'Planes got too big – some poor bloke tried to land a Constellation and left his undercarriage hanging off the sea wall.'

In the harbour swarm Chinese *sampans*, ferrying passengers and goods between town markets and ocean-going liners half-a-mile out. We're making slow progress through throngs of cycle-rickshaws, weaving in and out through the traffic. So we abandon the car at the Padang, the home of the Singapore Cricket Club with its grand Edwardian pavilion, and gawp at the imposing colonial structures around us – the Supreme Court, City Hall, Victoria Hall and mock-gothic St Andrew's Cathedral. Those Empire-builders knew a thing or two.

We hail a trio of rickshaws – a smart move. Charging fifty cents a mile, our toiling Chinese drivers pedal us wherever we want to go. They carry us to Empress Place, a landscaped area on the bank of the Singapore River, where we find a statue of Sir Stamford Raffles, Singapore's founder in 1819.

'When he landed,' our well-read friend informs us, 'the only people here were a bunch of pirates.' It's hard to imagine.

A Victorian cast-iron suspension bridge crosses the river – chock-a-block with teeming sampans. And it smells. Once sniffed, never forgotten.

The girls decide that's enough sightseeing for one morning – they're here for the shopping. We've been told that half the one-and-a-half million people here are in the retail trade. It's a duty-free port and prices are one-third of those in London. Even we blokes are interested.

We try the 'House of Tang' first. It's a five-storey Chinese lantern building and proclaims itself a 'treasure house of old-world loveliness'. It's all perfumed calm and full of jewellery, silverware, curios, embroidered linen, pewter and porcelain. There's carved teakwood furniture and camphor-wood chests – and many kinds of Chinese jade. All a bit rich for our taste so we go round the corner to Robinson's, an air-conditioned European-owned department store, to cool off and browse among the imported Rolex watches and Rollei cameras.

Next on our list is where you go, we're told, if you're young and don't have much money – Change Alley. We find it right by the harbour, crowded and humming. We're hustled by money-changers and jostled by children running around our legs. Between the open-fronted shops and the monsoon drain – the 'five-foot ways' – are laid out trays of intricate Japanese toys, gorgeous silks, colourfully dyed *batik* and cheap cottons. Costume jewellery and watches sell for a dollar or two but look like the genuine article. Both the trader and I know the haggling is a game, but I'm not entirely sure who's won when I end up buying a fake Swiss wristwatch with a date window. We're stopped by an Indian snake charmer who takes our cents and plays his pipe. Out of its rope-work basket, and apparently entranced, sways a hooded cobra. The girls edge away but we lads try to appear nonchalant and stand our ground.

It's time for a spot of lunch. Shall it be the Goodwood Hotel for a traditional British roast? Or Fosters, specialising so our guidebook says, in steaks flown in from Australia? Or we could blow out on *smörgåsbord* at the Raffles Hotel after a few Singapore Slings. Then there's the Javanese *rijstaffel* at the Cockpit if we are really feeling flush. But we're not – so we go for the Mont d'Or on Orchard Road, where there's air-conditioning, mulligatawny soup and beans on toast.

We stroll back to the Padang and drive 6 miles west to the Haw Par Villa and Tiger Balm Gardens. Our fount of all knowledge speaks up again.

'Haw Par ... they're the guys who invented Tiger Balm, aren't they? Made a fortune out of the stuff. Supposed to cure everything from torn muscles to snake bite. Stinks like hell, though.'

We meander round acres of hillside carved into bizarre grottoes and caves, and gardens full of grotesque concrete scenes from the gorier episodes of Chinese mythology. Worth visiting – just the once, we reckon. We're glad when a smiling Malay turns up on a bicycle, with a cold-box of Magnolia ice-cream.

We stay out west and sit outside The Gap, a restaurant on Marina Hill, looking down on the city lights and harbour. Over a Tiger beer or two we watch the sun set. At six-thirty prompt it flares over Sumatra in the west, flooding the clouds with gold, and then goes down like a trap-door.

What shall we do this evening? We decide against a film at any one of two dozen air-conditioned cinemas, and agree to save the restaurants of Chinatown for another time. We've missed the horse racing at Paya Lebar but we've been told Bugis Street's a must. We're not sure why – the guidebook just says *bugis* were piratical seafarers from Sulawesi. But it's on our way home and we find it one block from Nicoll Highway and the sea, surrounded by Chinese, Hindu and Buddhist temples. It's full of bars, cafes and eating stalls and we sit on clattering chairs at a table on the pavement, by the inevitable monsoon drain, and have another Tiger beer with plates of noodles and seafood. This is certainly a popular spot, and raucous gangs of sailors, airmen and soldiers are gathering around us.

Before long, we know why all these lads are here. From the top of the street comes a parade of stunning and exotic creatures, swinging their hips and moving to the music from the cafes. The crowd of servicemen goes wild. We're clearly at a loss, and a naval rating enjoys enlightening us.

'They ain't girls – they're *kaitais*, You know, blokes in drag.'

Some drag! These exquisite young men have women's figures. Dressed up and painted to the nines, the luscious lovelies strut their stuff for all they're worth.

It's bizarre to find this den of iniquity among the sacred temples. Do the strict Singapore authorities tolerate it here so that they can keep these lady-boys under their watchful eye? We certainly can't keep our eyes off them – they're weirdly fascinating.

After a while, it's time for home and I point the car eastwards for Changi. Out in the Straits, kerosene lamps are twinkling on the *kelongs*, long lines of fish-traps on poles. It's a romantic drive in the black tropical night, with cicadas calling and the scent of oleander on the air. Until, that is, over from Sumatra rolls the storm to end all storms. In no time at all the road's an impassable flood, visibility's nil and the windscreen wipers give up. We have no choice but to sit in the car and melt.

Eventually, the downpour relents enough for us to crawl home through the gloom and I drop off my passengers – all except one. For an hour or so, a pretty blonde WRAF officer and I enjoy each other's company in the steamy leather-upholstered privacy of the Riley.

I'm brought down to earth with our crew's first route trip, to Kuching, where we see the Borneo front-line up close.

We take off early. The bus calls by the Mess at 0430 – it's dark and chilly and after the flight briefing nobody feels much like talking over breakfast at the Changi Creek hotel. At this ungodly hour I can leave the grilled kidneys. With a load of snoozing soldiers, the Argosy takes off before the dawn that comes up in all its glory as we climb out over the South China Sea. Even through bleary eyes it's an uplifting sight and the first cup of coffee from the AQM makes me feel human at last.

It's just over two hours to Kuching. We skirt a couple of islands and dog-leg round Tanjong Datu headland – all Indonesian – and then turn south to the Sarawak coast. Two hills guide us nicely over the swamps and river deltas down to the town, just 10 miles inland, straddling the Sarawak River. The airfield's 5 miles further south and not much more than 20 miles from the border. We make a straight-in approach to the single runway, park the aircraft on a crowded dispersal and take our bearings.

It's a thriving commercial airport with terminal buildings. The civvie control tower's a hut on sticks and Military Ops are in corrugated iron constructions – hot as ovens. We make our report and file our return flight-plan in another hut full of RAF radio operators in contact with up-country bases. It's suspected that Indonesians will try to infiltrate the Kuching base and the Ops Officer has been issued with a pistol and the NCOs have .303 rifles and Sterling sub-machine-guns.

We're told there's been heavy action down on the frontier and we'll have casualties to take back to Changi Hospital – the helicopters are expected within the hour. While the Argosy's being refuelled we take a look around.

Behind the Ops buildings are the living quarters – nothing but six-man tents, except for the 215 Squadron groundcrew 'Hilton'. They've made a hut out of the wooden box used to sea-freight a Whirlwind helicopter, cutting holes for the windows, slinging primitive bunks and draping the entrance with mosquito nets. In this the six of them, one for each trade, cheerfully sweat out their two weeks' detachment. Beyond them at 150 yards is the barbed wire and beyond that, the jungle starts and goes on, mile after mile to the horizon.

In a shed we find a canteen and cups of tea. We're surrounded by soldiers: 42 Commando, SAS, Marines – and Gurkhas.

'Those Gurkhas and their flippin' rum rations – they give more trouble than the bloomin' Indos,' complains a Marine. 'Don't reckon their ration's enough so they cook up extra stuff themselves. Got so high last week they kidnapped 60 Squadron's goat mascot – had a ruddy sacrifice and barbequed it.'

'I don't know,' says an RAF Sergeant, 'they're not that bad. They did invite 60 Squadron to the party. Anyhow, they're bloody good in a scrap.'

We ask him what it's like here.

'All right really, if you don't mind the wildlife. There was a bloody great python in the showers this morning – leering up from the duckboards. Mosquito nets work OK though, and ciggie smoke seems to keep the flying beasties away – except for the frog flies. Ever seen one? Looks like an overgrown bluebottle. You can tie a bit of thread round 'em, keep hold of the end, and watch 'em do aerobatics.'

And what else do they do off duty?

'Well, last night we had *Saturday Night and Sunday Morning* down at the airport terminal – they had to make the screen out of two bloody great sheets sewn together. A trip downtown's good for beer and grub, as long as you get back on camp before the curfew. The boss is a stickler for that. Then there's the girls at the Chinese Nurses' Home.' He leans forward, confidentially. 'And they've got a new VD clinic for the local dollies – that's got to be better for the lads.'

We find our way back to the Argosy, through the Whirlwind and Belvedere helicopters, the Hastings, Pioneer and Valetta transports, and the civilian Dakota, and clamber into the sweltering cabin. It's been a blunt introduction to Sarawak. Boss Leary takes extra care with the take-off – we're bringing back half-a-dozen bullet-ridden Gurkhas. One of them has apparently accounted for nine of the bad guys.

These shuttles to Kuching and the other Borneo bases are a large part of 215 Squadron's routine. The Argosy impresses everyone with its versatility in combining passenger and freight roles. This comes at a price for the perspiring groundcrew at Changi. Among the most arduous of jobs is the constant changing of the aircraft interior rig, which usually has to be done overnight. But at destination airfields from doors-open to doors-closed is just one hour and the loadies love it for its easy-access clam-shell doors.

Between trips I've found time to fall for Ginny, the pretty blonde, and in the Mess anteroom after the Autumn Dance I'm left in no doubt the feeling's mutual. She's impressed with the Riley too, and we plan an expedition – adventurous in more than one respect – to Malacca. Our chance comes over the public holiday weekend of Deepavali, the Hindu Festival of Lights in late November. It's an opportunity for a spot of rest and recuperation, and after the heat and hell of Borneo and the frantic life of Changi, we're ready for some of it.

> Temple Hill Officers' Mess
> Royal Air Force
> Changi
> Singapore 17

20th November 1963

Dear Mother,

Thanks for the news from home. I hope you're feeling better after your rest in hospital. We've been having a bit of R and R ourselves. Last weekend was a public holiday and Ginny, my WRAF girlfriend, and I got away from the base (a bit like playing truant) and headed for Malacca. I wanted to see some more of this country – at ground level. Pat – that chap I shared digs with in Derby – he came along and brought Anne, the daughter of the Air Officer Admin here in Changi. Precious cargo ...

It pelted down some of the time but it was hot and sunny too. We took the scenic route across Singapore and passed houses up on piles (to keep the snakes out), and orchards and Chinese vegetable gardens surrounded by rubber trees and coconut palms. They're very keen to keep areas of unspoilt jungle, and Bukit Timah's one of the best, they say. We didn't stop at the Kranji War Cemetery (all elegant white marble, overlooking the sea) because we were there earlier this month for the Remembrance Day Parade. I have to say that the thought of all those World War II victims with no graves was pretty sad.

We had to cross the Causeway over the Straits to Johore Bahru on the Malay peninsula. As well as the road, it carries rail, water and telephone lines so we'd all be a bit stuck without it. Singapore's in the Malaysian Federation so we drove straight into Johore but weren't too sure what kind of a welcome to expect. You'll remember, Mother, that the whole Malayan Emergency began right here in 1948 and that thousands died – not only the Chinese Communists but locals, too. And I've found out that terrorism went on in Johore longer than anywhere else. It only ended three years ago and the Communist leader, Chin Peng, has never surrendered. The *Straits Times* here says that because he was an ally in the war, he reckoned he was promised a place in the Malayan government. They're actually still looking for him and his mates, so we were a bit nervous driving on the jungle roads.

The roads were good, though – a bit stony and pretty narrow, especially when I had to steer round a bullock cart – which was often. Odd beasts, bullocks – all humps and horns. They pull these carts on wheels 5 feet across, and the canopies over the top are really something – like rattan roofs, painted green, gold or blue with a red stripe down the middle. They bend up at the front like the corners of a pagoda, and a convoy of half-a-dozen of these contraptions, carrying pineapples and bananas, is quite a sight. It's a toss-up which is more dangerous – swinging the wheel to avoid the carts, or getting a good camera angle for the girls.

I'm enclosing some pictures for your classroom of the rubber plantations. You can see the spiral gash in the trunks and the way the latex is channelled into half coconut shells. The coast road we wanted turned off from the main highway to Kuala Lumpur and the jungle just went on for ever – we could hear all the wildlife buzzing and screeching away. We stopped now and again at roadside kiosks for chunks of mango and watermelon and they also had dusty old bottles of Guinness, of all things! Warm stout, anyone?

The *kampongs* (villages – I know the Malay word because the squadron's adopted one near Changi) are dotted here and there among pineapple and rice fields and water-buffalo wander about all over the place. Just short of Malacca, we stopped off at one *kampong* – not much more than a single street of bamboo huts with banana leaf or corrugated iron roofs. The Malays seemed very amused that we wanted to take snaps of them doing their laundry at the communal well! There were two big rivers to cross, both by chain ferries – motorized pontoons just big enough for two or three cars. Or in the case of one crossing, the Riley and a pair of water-buffalo taking the dry route. After the monsoon rains the rackety diesels struggled a bit against the flow. A great ride for 50 cents (about a bob) a go.

It took us eight hours to do the 200-odd miles, but it was fantastic. So was Malacca, where the Malays reckon their history began. We read in a book that a Hindu prince, fleeing from Sumatra over six centuries ago, lay down to rest under a Melaka tree and decided to stay. Well, it's as likely as anything else, isn't it? Anyhow, the Chinese, Portuguese and Dutch thought it a pretty useful place too, with its spices and gold. The British eventually got their hands on it around the end of the 18th century, and of course, got the spelling wrong.

In the town centre we could have been in Holland – if it weren't for the heat, the smell and the Queen Victoria Fountain in Dutch Square. The book said the bricks and tiles were all brought out as ballast in the ships that went back loaded with the riches of the East Indies.

We found rooms in a government resthouse – colonial-style lodgings for itinerant Brits, comfortable and good value, too. No air-conditioning, but the big ceiling fans did a good job. The girls were a bit put out by the size of the house-lizards in their room. The ones in the Changi *bashas* are called *chitchaks* or geckos and are only 4 inches long. They're great at just sitting quietly on the walls or ceilings till some winged creature comes along and then it's, whoomph – supper!

On Saturday, we spent hours rubber-necking around the old port (once the largest in Asia), the temples and fortifications – and Chinatown, of course. You'd love the spice shops – they're cool, and full of the scent of cardomom and cloves. Everywhere we looked, there was colour – red (lucky for the Chinese), green on the bullock carts, blue, white and black lacquer on the shop fronts and gold on the temples. People were more easy-going than in Singapore and we needn't have worried about our welcome.

The trip round the harbour in a sampan was wonderful. We sat in state while a Chinese boatman pushed us in and out among the other boats using one oar at the stern. Our oiled-paper sunshades came in handy and we watched the scenery go by – ancient, ramshackle Dutch wharves and rickety warehouses overhanging the water – decidedly whiffy, I have to say. Those old European matelots really had guts to make it all the way out here, year after year in their cockleshell ships.

We ate on Millionaire's Row a couple of times but don't worry, we didn't spend all our pay. It's Herrenstraat in Dutch, built by the descendants of prosperous plantation owners – Chinese men who had married Malay wives. They concocted their own spicy dishes, too – less fiery than the Indian curries, and they went down well with Tiger beer. We certainly needed a walk after that lot and I'm sure you can imagine what it was like, strolling under the stars among the frangipani trees ... It was hard to have to head back to Singapore on Sunday. We felt almost overwhelmed by the sights and smells and the heat and humidity, but we wouldn't have missed it for the world.

I'll write again when I get the chance. Keep smiling!

Love, Rog

PS. Pat's got back to find an envelope full of postcards from his mother. She's addressed them all to herself, and written on each one, 'Dear Mother, I am alive and well' – with instructions to fill in the date and send one once a month!

In the cool night air of Temple Hill, the sparkling waters of the Straits and the glare of Singapore behind me, I listen to the duty *chitchak* clicking on the wall above my bed and think again about those warm and promising kisses under the flickering harbour lights. Rested and recuperated, all's well.

Had I any hint of what lay round the corner, I might not have slept a wink.

CHAPTER FIVE

'Mayday – Mayday – Mayday'

T he Argosy was designed to be a medium freighter-coach, not a heavy lifter. However, the Army insisted that the floor be strengthened to carry a heavy stressed platform (HSP) for an armoured car. The reinforced steel added a weight penalty of 10,000 lb, a handicap that dogged the aircraft throughout its service life. There were from time to time rumours of an upgrade of engine to the more powerful version of the Dart, which might have brought the aircraft's performance at least up to specification. In the event, there's no record an HSP was ever dropped, but many medium stressed platforms (MSP) were, carrying a Land Rover and trailer, or a small tractor.

We were able to drop a pair in a 'daisy chain' in which the first platform deployed, pulling the second one out after it. As the first load moved towards the rear door, the control-column was moved firmly forward, with a rapid switch to aft as it went over the sill, and a further rapid fore-and-aft for the second. The navigator downstairs pulled a handle to release the load, and then watched the platforms rumble out. Once started, the process was unstoppable.

An MSP daisy chain dropping exercise is scheduled for two crews of 215 Squadron on the morning of 25 November, up at Kuantan, an air-field in East Malaya. But on take-off, the first aircraft away loses the over-wing hatches to the dinghy stowage – they fly over the tailplane and fall onto the runway. The two 32-seater dinghies, with their gas-bottles and canopies, stay lodged in their wing stowage. The Control Tower warns the crew, who abort the mission, and the Argosy lands safely and returns to dispersal. A modification has been carried out on these hatches just yesterday and clearly, all is not well.

I am co-pilot with Boss Leary and the usual crew plus a rigging party of eight soldiers, in the second aircraft. Following the earlier mishap, Mister

Howarth and the groundcrew now look for themselves at the hatches on our aircraft, XP446. Each has a small observation window to check the latches for correct fastening. All seems in order and we're cleared for the sortie.

We climb on board and find the two MSPs, with Land Rover and trailer, almost completely filling the freight compartment, leaving just enough room for the rigging party to sit in their canvas bucket-seats along the side wall. Close to the maximum all-up-weight, the Argosy rolls ponderously out to the runway. It's a fine, clear morning – there's been thunder and lightning every afternoon this month, but we'll be back well before the storms build up. I'm looking forward to a pleasant trip and a new experience.

The take-off run is normal but as the Argosy lifts off, there's vibration through the control column. As we climb away from the end of the runway and over the sea, the shaking gets worse. Could the elevator counterweight be shearing? I've heard this is a possibility with the Argosy. In any event, we're all used to the natural flexing of the Argosy and XP446 continues its climb. The water-methanol boosting is turned off and the flaps retracted. Under climbing power, course is set for the Kong Kong beacon just north of Changi and I switch the radio to Changi Approach.

Then, without warning, at about 1,800 feet, the controls start to shudder violently and the aircraft's nose rears up alarmingly. The skipper reacts immediately – shoving the control column fully forward and furiously winding the elevator trimmers. Still the nose rises. This is serious.

Unknown to us, the dinghy hatches have been sucked away at the point of maximum lift on take-off and the dinghies have inflated and burst out of their stowage. One of them has wrapped itself around the tailplane.

The aircraft's nose then drops sickeningly and the Argosy, all 97,000 lb of it – soldiers, MSPs, aircrew and all – performs an aerobatic manoeuvre forbidden in this aeroplane. It's called a 'bunt' – a negative-G outside loop. Outside, the deflated dinghy, punctured by its own gas bottle, is beating the ailerons to death. But all we in the cockpit know is that the elevators are out of commission and the aircraft is going exactly where it wants – porpoising across the sky, regardless of the Boss's battle with the controls.

There's worse to come. The left wing drops and the aircraft plunges into an uncontrollable left-hand spiral dive. We're now descending near to vertical. I stare petrified at the rocks and seaweed straight down below in the blue waters of the South China Sea. I sit rigid in my seat waiting to meet my Maker. Time is frozen, oblivion is imminent and there's nothing I can do.

But the skipper calls for power off and Mister Howarth, imperturbable as ever, pulls the throttles fully back. Bathed in sweat, the Boss hauls back on the control column and somehow heaves the heavy aeroplane out of its screeching dive at 400 feet. Miraculously, it's pointing straight back at the runway we've just left – but in the opposite direction – and just about maintaining height.

In my earphones, the voice of the Boss: 'Co-pilot, send a distress message on Changi local – ask for a downwind landing.'

'Roger, Skipper.' I switch to Changi local and thumb the transmit button.

'Mayday – Mayday – Mayday. This is four-four-six. Position two miles north-east of Changi at 400 feet. Request emergency landing on runway two zero. Over.'

There's not much we can do if they refuse.

'Roger four-four-six. Beware two aircraft taking off.'

Almost instantly, two Royal Navy Buccaneers flash by, taking extreme and urgent evasive action as the Argosy barrels down into their flight path. Out of the corner of my eye, I see a rescue helicopter that has already been scrambled in response to our 'Mayday'.

Meanwhile, the skipper has calmly instructed the doubtless bewildered and terrified rigging party and AQM downstairs to prepare for a possibly heavy landing. He calls for the landing checks.

'Undercarriage down.' I push the button with trepidation. Three red lights – three greens!

'Landing flap, Co – but be ready to take them up again.' He's concerned that the flaps might disturb the aircraft trim. They don't, and as we come to the bottom of our glide-slope the runway threshold slips under our wheels.

We bump down. But a downwind landing at full take-off weight is not standard practice – and we're going very fast.

'Props to fully-fine.' The disking propellers bite against the slipstream.

Braking aggressively, he manages to pull up before the trenches at the far end of the runway – trenches dug for maintenance work, not as speed traps for wayward Argosies.

With deep sighs of relief, we turn and backtrack along the runway as Air Traffic informs us there's something hanging off the tailplane. We taxi back to a welcoming committee of Squadron Commander, Engineering Officer, concerned groundcrew and several sightseeing aircrews.

Ashen-faced, we clamber down the ladders and join the shaken soldiers out beside the aircraft. For the first time we understand what has happened to us. There's a burst thirty-two-seater dinghy, with canopy and gas bottle, wrapped around the starboard elevator. The gas bottle has damaged the tail-boom and the elevator. The aircraft is festooned with nylon cord and the dinghy's mooring lanyard is stretched from hatch to tailplane, trailing through the split in the starboard wing flaps. It was our luck that the Argosy's split elevator meant the left-hand side was still working – that was almost certainly what saved us.

Impassively, Mister Howarth reports that the brakes have over-heated and the aircraft accelerometer is reading plus six and minus five G – way outside the limits. Incredibly, we've pulled enough G to worry a fighter pilot. It's a tough old bird, the Argosy.

The Boss lines up the propellers, in his usual unhurried way. Rev, the navigator, throws up over the starboard undercarriage. After helping to write an incident report, I go off to the Officers' Mess bar for something to settle the nerves. In the afternoon the skipper joins another crew for a trip to Kuantan with another Argosy – after making extensive examination of the hatch fastenings. Sergeant Bateman, the AQM, requests a transfer to passenger aircraft – and gets it.

Flying for me is never the same again. From now on I'm fearful that any flexing of the Argosy in turbulence might turn into another sickening bunt and spiral dive. Sitting in the co-pilot's seat in thunderstorms for hours on end becomes an even more anxious business. But when I've got a reassuring grasp on the control column myself, it's fine. So in good service tradition, I press on.

A couple of days later, in the Mess I meet the Air Traffic controller who received my 'Mayday'. He says that he's never heard anyone sound so calm and professional under stress. Calm and professional – I like that. I buy him another Tiger.

I wasn't allowed to sit around contemplating eternity for long. Throughout December, 215 Squadron and its sister squadrons were at full stretch supporting operations in Borneo. Body bags were a common cargo on the Labuan and Kuching runs. Indonesian ground fire hit an Auster of 7 Flight Army Air Corps, killing a Wing Commander padre, and two soldiers were drowned trying to rescue supplies from the river at Bintulu. On one Labuan shuttle, all we carried was the coffin containing one of them, a Marine Sergeant Major who'd been in the water for a week. We could carry nothing else because of the stench, which was such that the whole crew sat on the flight deck with the hatch closed for the entire three-and-a-half hour flight.

On 7 December a crew was called to Brunei in a great hurry, taking a full load of sixty-nine troops and their kit. The mission was to reinforce the Royal Leicesters, who had lost a platoon when 200 Indonesians came across the border. The Argosy landed safely on the short runway, off-loaded the troops and took the wounded on board. The Royal Leicesters' Captain wanted the crew to take the bodies of two soldiers that had been in the river for three days, followed by two days in a shed. The coffins lids were nailed down but were bursting open with the putrefaction and simply could not be carried on the same aeroplane as a bunch of casevacs. They had to wait.

Tom Sneddon was on this flight and it affected him deeply. We never knew whether the bodies made it back to Singapore or were buried in Brunei. He wrote home: 'How many people in Britain have the least idea of the real shooting war going on out here in Borneo?'

By this time there were about 6,000 British troops on the Indonesian frontier fighting off guerrilla attacks. Russian-built Il-28 bombers were making sorties across the border and the up-country airstrips were being beaten up daily by American-supplied Mitchells and Mustangs. Just before Christmas, 128 guerrillas attacked a Malay base at Kalabakan near Tawau in eastern Sabah, 20 miles inside the border, killing eight Royal Malayan Regiment soldiers. In a counter-attack the 1st/10th Gurkhas killed or captured the raiders, and the identification of twenty-one of them as regular Indonesian Marines showed that the campaign was intensifying.

On Christmas Eve, 48 Squadron hosted a party at the children's home they'd recently adopted. Every officer paid five dollars a month into a kitty to provide some fun for the kids. We on 215 Squadron gave a Christmas party for all ranks, and it coincided with the Station Commander's tour of his domain, as judge of the Inter-Unit Best-Decorated Bar Competition. He carried his own quarter-pint tankard – anything larger at each stop would have left him legless. The 215 Squadron entry was an Egyptian tomb, built out of chicken wire and plaster and unnervingly realistic. The entrance was a mock fireplace, which revolved as the Group Captain approached, to reveal a full-size sarcophagus complete with mummy. The CO was suitably taken aback when the mummy sat up and greeted him warmly. Aircraftman Mike Robson spent the rest of the day and evening swathed in increasingly disintegrating bandages. The New Zealanders of 41 Squadron won the competition with their representation of a cave complex back home. They'd commandeered the concrete bunker next-door, complete with machine-gun post on top. It was dark as hell and the booze was lethal.

On Christmas Day the Sergeants' and Airmen's Messes invaded the Officers' Mess at 1100 and then the officers returned the compliment from 1230 to about 1530. It was all downhill from there.

Christmas dinner at Temple Hill was in full white sharkskin mess kit, and a bunch of nurses had been invited from the Sisters' Mess. Chinese crackers and water pistols were the order of the day, and bread rolls, grapes and oranges flew about the room. The finale was provided by seven of us standing on the table, under intense fire, bellowing '*Cwm Rhondda*' above the general din. Unable to come up with an encore, we left the nurses to their own devices, and retired with our girls to the Officers' Club, with its band and cabaret.

While all that was going on, the Flight Commander, Boss Leary, my captain of the past five months, flew his Argosy with mail and greetings to Kuching, Brunei and Labuan – an eight-hour round trip. Brunei was a diversion to pick up a critically ill soldier. Sadly, he died on the approach to Labuan, and this made the Christmas festivities there somewhat muted. The body was put in a bag and taken back to Changi strapped in a seat. Such is the stark reality of active service.

The Boss takes another co-pilot on that trip. At the beginning of December I've changed crews – a routine event but one I have difficulty in coming to terms with. These four extraordinary months as a crew – with the relief of Djakarta, the Labuan missions and our close shave with the dinghy hatches – seem to have taken me from rookie trainee to a campaigner of sorts. I sit by the Officers' Club pool, under the stars with Ginny. I'm still alive and reckon that whatever comes, I am up for it.

CHAPTER SIX

Down in the Jungle

Along way from home, serving men naturally become a little sentimental at Christmas time. That clearly could not be said for President Sukarno, who stepped up the pace of his *Confrontasi* with a vengeance.

Following the December attack at Kalabakan, five Hastings, four Argosies and two Beverleys promptly flew reinforcements from Singapore to Labuan – 380 troops and their equipment – in just twelve hours. The men were fed in the RAF field kitchen and dispatched to Tawau within three hours in five Beverley sorties. The next day, six Argosies and three Hastings arrived, similarly loaded, and seven Beverley sorties took them to Tawau. In all, 1,500 soldiers were carried the 1,300 miles to the front line in two days.

When the Minister of Defence, Peter Thorneycroft, visited RAF Labuan in January, he found twelve transports and a Shackleton operating from the airfield, together with four fighters and fifteen helicopters. The number of men had risen to nearly 500, many still housed six to a tent – a feast for the mosquitoes. Around 1,100 aircraft movements were recorded in the month, including 100 at night.

The countries of South East Asia were worried that the mounting tension might destabilise the whole area. It was only a couple of years before that sixteen years of bloodshed among the Dutch and Indonesians had ended. In Tokyo, there were talks about negotiations between Indonesia and Malaysia, and a tentative ceasefire was brokered. The newly established Royal Malaysian Air Force (RMAF) now had a permanent detachment of two Twin Pioneers at Labuan. Flying at treetop height over the border villages, they braved the Indonesian machine-guns to sell the ceasefire through loudspeakers to locals and Indo guerrillas alike. But it didn't hold. Far from withdrawing, the Indonesians stepped up the force, frequency and distribution of their raids.

The pattern was that bands of press-ganged tribesmen from Kalimantan, armed with *parangs*, and strengthened by about 1,500 Sarawak

Communist Chinese, would spearhead the attacks with Indonesian regulars supporting in the rear. The objective seemed to be to terrorise the native population – not difficult to do. It was well known in the jungle villages that in his anti-Communist purges, Sukarno had led the massacre of over 300,000 Chinese.

In response, British forces developed a system of forts and strong points, each protected by an outer picket line. Infantry would man these posts, ready to be lifted forward by helicopter at a moment's notice. Gurkhas were a key element. They were fierce fighters with jungle skills matched by those of the SAS, and units from both forces together watched over favourite Indonesian border-crossings.

The British helicopter force was doubled in February by RNAS Whirlwinds from off-shore carriers and by twin-rotor heavy-lifting Belvederes, 'Flying Longhouses', sent out from Odiham. The helicopters took on all manner of tasks – abseiling reinforcements in and winching casualties out, whisking platoons, Commanders and messages from one post to another, and resupplying food, dry clothing and ammunition.

Border penetration by the British troops was strictly prohibited and despite intense provocation, there was no hot pursuit. The frequent attacks could be contained as long as the Indonesians didn't commit their regulars or their potentially massive air support. But it was all most uncomfortable for the British soldiers, under the dark jungle canopy, bitten by insects and snakes, in the pouring rain and steamy heat. It was also dangerous, the patrols being vulnerable to ambush at any time by guerrillas wielding knives and carbines.

Relaying radio messages for the low-flying helicopters and making drops from several hundred feet, we transport crews were relatively safe with four Rolls-Royces or Bristols to take us home. It was time to find out what it was really like down there – time for our Jungle Survival Training.

Early on a Monday morning we report to the Far East Survival and Parachute School for our seven-day course. The school, in its collection of *basha* huts down on Changi Beach, is run by half-a-dozen hard-as-nails RAF Physical Education Branch instructors, known familiarly as 'phyzzies'. Their officer is naturally nicknamed Jungle Jim.

We trainees are three-dozen aircrew drawn from all the Singapore squadrons, an assortment of officers and NCOs thrown in together at the deep end. Gathered in the classroom for briefing, we hear out on the verandah, the clucking of chickens.

'That, gentlemen, is your lunch,' says Jungle Jim.

In teams of seven, we're shown how to build an oven from hot stones buried in sand. So far so good, but it soon dawns on us that killing and preparing the meat is down to us – and the ill-fated fowls. Some do better than others. First, as they say, catch your chicken.

'It's all right, chaps – leave it to me.' A portly Argosy captain chases a squawking bird, trips at full speed and falls headlong on the unfortunate creature, trapping and slaughtering it in one fell swoop.

We've been issued with *parangs*, cutting knives with 2 feet-long blades.

'*Bansai!*' Brandishing his, Bob Hodges, a young and nimble Sergeant AQM, corners one and with a single swipe, succeeds in cutting his fingers almost to the bone. He's our first casualty.

Our team's blessed with an AQM from a farm in Wales. Taff Howell is experienced in these matters and before we know it, our lunch is caught in his powerful hands and humanely throttled. He can cook too, and although a bit gristly, our chicken-in-sand meal is better than most. But there's a lot of blood and grease around and those of us mistakenly in best khaki drill wish we weren't.

The next day, dressed in our oldest jungle-green flying-suits, we're briefed on the flora and fauna of the jungle – their edibility and conversely, their inclination to bite. It sounds like there's plenty to eat – shoals of fish and flocks of birds. Not so appealing are the beetles, grubs, grasshoppers, lizards and snakes. For the vegetarian there's breadfruit, sweet potatoes, bamboo shoots and coconut.

'But watch out,' we're advised, 'for the strychnine plants, physic nuts and castor-oil beans. They, and a lot of other stems, leaves and roots can leave you dead within hours – or bring on diarrhoea so violent that you wish you were.'

We're taught about the different jungle terrains. In the *ulu*, the usually uninhabited and exposed country up in the headwaters of the rivers, we're warned to look out for blowpipe hunters. In the *ladang*, jungle cleared for cultivation – often *padi* (rice) up in the highlands – we'd find longhouses and people. In the *belukar*, abandoned *ladang* where the undergrowth has grown back into thick secondary jungle, we should be more likely to find animals, fruit and maybe vegetables. But hacking through it is hell. And then there's primary jungle, the *bundu* – miles of it, where the trees are tall and the canopy intact, and not much grows below.

Snakes get a whole lesson to themselves. There are over forty types on Singapore Island and many more in the jungle. Generally speaking, we're told, they're not aggressive, except for the King cobra. They only attack you if you attack them – by accidentally stepping on them, for instance. Tom and I remember that the next morning when we're the first to arrive at the gates of the Survival School.

'Bloody hell, Rog, don't look now but I think there's something dangerous up in that tree.' I look up.

'You could be right there, Tom.'

There's a massive snake coiled round a low branch, between us and the school.

'Do you think it's seen us? What was it they told us to do?'

'Don't do anything aggressive,' says Tom, 'like treading on it.'

Trying to look friendly, we ease past the monster – it must be all of 20 feet long. In the safety of the classroom, Jungle Jim tells us that the python's actually an old chum,. It's been around for years and is known to the phyzzies as Peter. We smile wanly.

Today, we practise building jungle shelters, from the simple one-person A-frame type to the more complex seven-man lean-to hut. We use banana leaves, and bamboo in pre-cut lengths – not, we suspect, so readily available out in the jungle.

We're briefed on the next stage: four days and three nights as teams in an area of jungle 90-odd miles up into Malaya near Mersing. We're told that the training is to prepare us for the hopefully unlikely event of crash-landing during an operation. According to the manual: *The jungle does not offer much in the way of forced-landing areas.* From what we've seen, they can say that again. We are advised: *Look for beaches, clearings, paddy fields, lakes and rivers – do not land on treetops.* So far, over Borneo we've seen precious little but trees. Therefore, not many of us take this training too seriously and that evening in the bar, we're full of bravado.

But next morning, as we arrive clutching our 'few personal items' – cigarettes and matches, boiled sweets, and condoms for protection of a sensitive part from leeches – there's an unexpected twist.

'Good morning, gentlemen. Welcome to the practical part of the course. At no extra expense we're able to offer you a further three days – an escape and evasion exercise.' Jungle Jim's announcement strikes fear in our hearts. 'After the four days' survival you'll be let loose in the *bundu* to make your way back down the Peninsula to Singapore. Brawny blokes of the RAF Regiment will pursue you and do their level best to bag you. They will then practise their renowned interrogation techniques. You lucky people, you.'

Blast – we thought we'd got out of that bit. We've heard from Geoff Walker, who has done it, that this is no picnic. The Regiment, known disrespectfully to us as 'Rock Apes', is given a helping hand by Australian pilots from Butterworth, who roar across the treetops in Sabrejets laying down flares. Geoff got as far as the Straits of Johore, but got caught trying to swim across and was locked up in an old Jap bread oven. The Regiment put wet cloths on his head and beat a tattoo on the oven with a stick all night. He says that he didn't break, but saw a famously tough Sergeant who did. Hardened campaigner though he was, he came out shaking and in tears.

We smile grimly and board the bus for the *bundu*. The Smith & Wesson .38 side-arms at our hips don't help our peace of mind. They've been issued 'in case of contact with terrorists'.

After a hot and bone-shaking three hours in a 3-tonner, we tumble out into a forest clearing by the east-coast road. At ten-minute intervals, teams set off into the bush in varying directions. There's a phyzzie with each group, leading the way and marching along a well-defined track. What's all the fuss about? But soon the track peters out and we're making slow progress through thick undergrowth, taking turns with the *parang* to cut a path through tough, rope-like liana creepers, giant tree-ferns, bamboo clumps and nettle-trees that set our skin on fire. Visibility's no more than 20 yards, so we go on a compass bearing, clambering up and down the steep gullies that bar our path, making no more than a couple of hundred yards in an hour. There's not that much kit to carry, but the damned pistol seems to weigh a ton. We've been issued with poncho capes, but the flipping rain bounces up off the ground and gets underneath them – we're soaked to the skin. When it's not raining it's blooming hot and there's no cooling breeze down under the canopy. Squelching through streams and swamp, our jungle-boots get sodden and heavy too. There are ants everywhere and they bite. Blimey – this is absolutely bloody awful.

After some hours, we come out into primary jungle, where the canopy is so thick and so far above our heads that it's dark as hell. With less undergrowth, the going's easier but we're still clambering hand-over-hand up steep slopes and plunging headlong down the other side. And it's raining again.

We stop in the afternoon to set up camp, choosing a glade by a stream for drinking and washing. We make sure there's no dead animal rotting up-stream and that we're above flood level. The water can rise 30 feet overnight in the storms and we don't fancy being swept away in a raging torrent.

A crew sleeping-platform has to be built before dark. There's plenty of bamboo and creeper, but sure enough, cutting it out here is far from easy. After much cursing, we manage to get some sort of structure up. It's raised on poles off the wet ground, and away, we hope, from the snakes, beetles and ants – nightmarish soldier ants an inch-and-half long. They're not the ones that bite though – it's the little quarter-inch devils that eat you alive.

With no time left now to look for those promised shoals of fish and bunches of breadfruit, we make some semblance of a fire from the sopping undergrowth and cook up our survival rations. Famished, we wolf the tasteless mess, washing it down with muddy water flavoured with halazone purifying tablets. Our phyzzie has insisted that we take water from a stagnant puddle – 'for experience'.

The smoke from the fire keeps the worst of the mosquitoes away and wet, muddy and dead tired we crash out in our seven-man shelter. I doze off, but suddenly I'm bolt-upright with a fierce pain in my crutch. Leaping out of the *basha* I rip down my soggy drawers – and in the light of the embers see a bloody great leech hanging off my scrotum.

I'm shocked and horrified. The foul creature's got its teeth into me – it's sucking my blood and already the size of a tennis-ball. I remember what we've been told to do. Never pull them off – that'll leave the little blighter's jaws in you and the bite will fester. You burn them off with a lighted fag-end or squirt them with iodine. I don't fancy the red-hot cigarette option on the balls, so go for the iodine. A couple of squirts does it. The wretched thing falls off, still swollen with blood, and drops down into my blasted trouser leg.

God, I hate this place.

We don't get a lot of sleep the first night, but at least we've got each other's company – as on the second night, when after another day's forced march, we pair up in smaller bamboo and liana lean-tos. But on the third evening we make single A-frame shelters and really find out what a night in the jungle's all about.

It's been quite a pleasant day, relatively speaking. The rain's given us a break. The dawn was also magnificent. I noticed that the sun doesn't come up in the jungle, it comes down. The first rays hit the tree canopy and then creep down the massive trunks until they reach you in your *basha* and warm you up until you're ready for action. On the march again, we found, after more hours of jungle-bashing, a clear stretch of river and threw off all our clothes, submerging ourselves like so many hippos in the cool, sun-dappled water. No leeches here in the fast-flowing stream, and to hell with the hornets and sandflies. It was absolutely bloody marvellous, so we set up camp and for our meal had some of those promised fish – Taff's huge hands made great traps. Just for a while, the jungle was a great place.

But then we go to bed. We've been forced to set up our bivouacs at least 20 yards apart. That's a long way in the jungle night – cold, damp with condensation, and noisy. The only animals we've seen on the whole trek have been a couple of gibbons, an outsize lizard, and a few birds. But tonight I hear screams and hooting, rattles and booming, rustles and slithering – the lot. Is something getting ready to pounce on me? Or creep up from underneath? Now the imagination really gets going. What about deadfall trees? We've been warned that when a dying jungle giant decides to fall, it drops like a thousand-ton brick. Bang – just like that. Did I check there were no tottering tree-trunks about to demolish my puny shelter? I'm in a cold sweat, not certain I'll ever see daylight again.

I nod off – only to be jolted awake by a fearsome racket in the undergrowth. Is this what a charging rhino sounds like? Nothing happens, the commotion subsides, and I try to drift off again. But, what seems only moments later, there's a blood-curdling scream. A human one for sure. Has the rhino come back? Once again silence descends.

From time to time I half wake to the crash of deadfalls out in the forest, but eventually the night passes. Still tired, wet and hungry, we cluster round the breakfast fire.

'Anyone else hear that rhino?'

'Rhino – what rhino? If you mean all that clattering about in the middle of the night, that was me,' mumbles Tom.

It turns out he had made himself a hammock from several parachute panels, with spreaders made from branches at either end lashed to tree trunks, and his poncho overhead for shelter. To avoid falling out, he'd strapped the parachute panels round his ankles, a device that worked well for half the night. But then the spreader at the head snapped, the whole contraption collapsed and he was left suspended, like a bat, by his feet.

'Was that you as well – yelling blue murder?'

It wasn't. A shame-faced Squadron Leader, who shall remain nameless, confesses that his arm, curled around the back of his neck, had gone to sleep. Suddenly waking up, and convinced that he was being strangled by a python, he had screamed in sheer terror.

Even more shame-faced we realise that, wild beasts or not, no one had had the nerve to move out of his A-frame to investigate.

For our sins, we now face the dreaded Escape and Evasion. But miraculously, the phyzzie receives a message on his short-wave radio. Reprieve! The exercise is cancelled. We cheer. The powers that be have decided that given the security situation, there's a real danger that we'd be mistaken for insurgents and shot.

It's a dishevelled and shambling crowd that treks out of the *bundu*. One by one we meet up with other teams and share stories.

'Did you catch anything to eat?'

'No bloody chance. Apart from some fish – which were great – we've seen nothing but birds and bats, and the odd monkey. They heard us lot coming and scarpered – except the flaming ants.'

'That's right, and we didn't even hear anything, except at night – what a row! And breadfruit? Ruddy monkeys didn't leave us any kind of fruit, did they?'

'Jungle Jim reckons he's smelled a tiger!'

But apart from attacks from thorns, ants and leeches, and the odd bruise or two, we're all in one piece.

The Malayan Army Captain on one crew seems to know the jungle better than the instructors do. He's found bananas and caught a terrapin that he's presented to Jungle Jim. He's also collected a score of Siamese fighting fish and reckons they'll fetch a dollar or more a piece in Changi Market.

Then – it happens. We're still in deep undergrowth, but on a well-marked trail and off our guard, when we hear a deep, menacing roar. Not 10 yards away in front of us on the path sits a very large tiger. Everyone freezes. Then Jungle Jim – his sense of smell proving alarmingly accurate – slowly draws out his revolver, aims between the animal's eyes and squeezes the trigger. But the gun fails to fire. At the same moment, there's another roar from further off – and lazily, the tiger gets up and trots off to join her mate.

We slowly let out our breath. 'Blimey Jim, that was a close call!'

'Sure was. Good thing the pistol didn't go off. Male tigers like their white meat.'

We make it to the *rendezvous* with the buses and there in the clearing, waiting for us, is the Magnolia Man on his bike with ice-cream, sodas and chilled fresh pineapple juice. We fall on his cold-box like wolves. The mysterious jungle telegraph has told him exactly when and where we'd turn up.

Showered, fed and rested, our rotted jungle clothing in the dustbin, we proud survivors gather in the Temple Hill bar. If we didn't treat the course seriously at the outset, we sure as hell do now. It's been at the very least a great adventure. The jungle is terrifying yet beautiful – and always uncomfortable. We agree that we're unlikely to put the training to much use – surviving a crash-landing in this terrain would be nigh-on impossible. But we've been given an inkling of what it must be like down there for the soldiers we drop to and we're in awe. We now know how wearying it is just staying alive, and that's without having to track, recce, carry a pack and rifle – and fight. Jungle Jim's told us a four-man patrol takes three days with their *parangs* to make a clearing for our airdrops. If we miss by 20 yards they abandon that container – the effort of cutting through the undergrowth is just not worth it, and it's probably up in the trees anyway. We'll remember that when we're next over the DZs.

Eventually, all aircrews go on the Survival Course, and some go on Sea Survival too. That involves bobbing about in a dinghy for some hours just over the horizon from Changi, waiting for rescue by helicopter, but it's cancelled when an infestation of sharks is sighted.

Many of us have fallen in love with the jungle. We organise barbeques up in the scrub by Jason's Bay near Mersing. The girls come along and – kind souls that they are – appear impressed by our expert knowledge of the hazards. The Magnolia Man turns up there too. Hired ramshackle motorboats from Changi Creek take us to outlying islands for jungle beach-picnics, but these aren't a great success. In the north-east monsoon of January to March, the water's stirred up into a muddy soup and in the dry season there are too many sandflies – and there's never a Magnolia Man.

At Kota Tinggi, 80 miles up-country, we find paradise lost. On the survival course we heard about some waterfalls in the area and with our newfound love of the jungle, set off in our cars to explore, me with the singles in the Riley and Horse and other marrieds and their families in Beetles and Jeeps. Parking by a roadside stall – and declining another invitation to buy warm Guinness – we trek into the *bundu*. Bypassing deadfall trees and crossing streams, we nearly stumble into an enormous spider's web, at least 4-feet-square, stretched across the track. In the middle, as big as a dinner plate and glaring at us, sits a long-legged, yellow spider. We put on a brave show for the women and children and break down the web to get past. After an hour, we come to a chain of waterfalls and pools – clear, cool and shady. Shangri-blooming-la! We swim, and laze on the rocks, picnicking on watermelons cooled in the stream – a million miles from strife. A durian tree shades us, its brown trunk rising above the scrub, but its big bunches of spiky fruit are out of reach. Just as well, as they stink to high heaven. The locals prize them, but they're a bit too exotic for our taste. We look out for all the wildlife that Jungle Jim said had been seen in the area – pigs, honey-bears, scaly anteaters and white rhino – but they keep their distance. He'd also alerted us to water-borne diseases such as leptospirosis. Happily, none of us ever developed the fever, violent headaches, and other distressing symptoms he listed.

Two or three glorious hours later, we trek out to find that the industrious spider has rebuilt its web. This time, we respectfully hack a way round it. We return here time and again, and never see anyone else there. It's our secret.

From time to time, the co-pilots and navigators of 215 Squadron found themselves uncomfortably close to the jungle, on ground operations. Geoff Walker – now known affectionately to all ranks as 'Duffy' – was the first to pack his combat kit and in March was posted to Tawau for four weeks as Air Liaison Officer. The Indonesians persisted in their guerrilla raids over the border just a mile or two away across the harbour, and one night, he was dragged in his pyjamas from his camp bed by the Sergeant

Major and shoved into a slit-trench. He was to defend the base with nothing but a pistol. When the order was given to fix bayonets, he knew things were serious. Gunfire crackled throughout the night and before the raiders were repulsed, his tent had been raked with bullets.

The same month, the first Argosy landed at Tawau, carrying fifty-one soldiers as reinforcements. The closeness of the border called for a tight approach, and the short and sloping runway meant the landing had to be tactical.

A tactical landing is where the aircraft is brought in steeply, just above the stall, with full flap and a good deal of power on – hanging, as it were, on the props. Power is cut at the last second and the Argosy drops in with a bump and subsequent heavy use of the brakes. Under particularly hefty boots they've been known to seize up, when the standard engineering procedure to free them is a sharp wallop with a large hammer. A tactical take-off is only slightly less hairy. Full water-methanol boosting is used to rotate at the earliest possible moment, and a period of straight-and-level just above the ground builds up sufficient speed, after a while, to climb away.

This first landing at Tawau was so tactical that the undercarriage lifted the perimeter fence out of the ground. Fortunately, it was made of light wooden pickets and a single strand of wire. The pilot happened to be the Squadron Commander.

The Argosies were now also flying regular shuttles to Brunei town airport, where the short-field capabilities of the aircraft again came into play. The runway was quite short and the luxuriant jungle came down to the perimeter fence. So it was one way in, over the sea, and the other way out. Again, the landing had to be tactical, as it was at neighbouring Seria. On both routes, sometimes three shuttles in a day, we ferried Gurkha troops whose main base was in Brunei.

Sometimes, they brought their families and, as if at home, the women would set out their primus stoves in the middle of the freight cabin. Unfortunately, they were not familiar with aircraft toilets, reasoning that any door would lead directly outside – to certain death. Our AQMs dealt with both situations with varying degrees of tact.

Our other regular jungle destination was Sibu in Sarawak, an airfield swarming with helicopters in support of the troops and their increasing jungle action. The first flight was in May, made by Boss Leary after one of his trial runs in a Beverley. The runway was tarmac, but only 1,500 yards long, and the landing was dangerous enough – tactical again – without the raised lip at the threshold waiting to take off the undercarriage if the touchdown fell short.

These shorter-field landings, at our limits, deepened our respect for the crews of Twin and Single Pioneers. They flew over the jungles and mountains and through the weather at 90 knots and at 1,000 feet. They operated in and out of cramped airstrips, usually of dirt with a foundation of wooden logs, quite often weakened by munching termites to the point of collapse. For us, these strips were reasonable dropping zones but for them, they were challenging tests of flying skill.

I land from a morning shuttle to Kuching at the end of May to be called to the Station Commander's office at Station Headquarters, alongside the Padang. On its coarse grass last weekend I was introduced by Duffy, himself an almost suicidally committed tackler, to the questionable pleasures of Far East rugby football. I was asked to stand in the Station XV line-out, where my height was supposed to make me a star. I coped with that, but not so well with the first scrum when the opposing hooker's knee came up and accidentally broke my nose. As I park alongside the scene, my mind's on that painful experience, rather than on possible reasons for being called to see the Station Commander this morning.

I've no fear of the man himself – Group Captain Brian Bennett AFC is popular with all ranks. He allocates secondary duties, such as Mess Secretary or captain of the Sub-Aqua Club, and it's possible that he has one for me. I understand the Station's looking for a new cricket captain, and I've done a reasonable job with the Station XI, opening the bowling with Taff. I'm certainly in no fear of being carpeted – I've done nothing wrong lately. I march in, stand to attention and salute.

'At ease, Annett. Please sit down.' This is the last thing I expected.

'I'm afraid I have some bad news.'

He hands me a small sheet of flimsy paper – a telegram. It's from my elder brother, telling me that my mother passed away just yesterday.

I go into the sort of shock that the mind and body reserve for such occasions and half hear the CO's condolences. He tells me that I'm booked on the evening Comet back to England on compassionate leave. The rest of the day's a blur. Ginny, who works in the Movements Section, processes my papers and checks me onto the flight. It helps to have her there.

Back in the chill of an English spring, I've gained several hours across the time zones but lost all orientation. My mother had been ill for some time and was waiting for an operation when I was posted last August. My brother has made all the arrangements and I am simply required to attend the funeral. I try to hide my broken nose and am determined not to weep in my RAF dress uniform – brought musty and creased out of storage to be pressed for the occasion. My grief is real but I've been away for almost a year and feel remote from the ceremony, the huddles of relatives and the sherry and sandwiches. When everyone has gone home and I can't sleep because of the jetlag, I feel pretty much alone – and guilty at not having written home more. To get back to a semblance of normality, I meet the regulars at the pub and even get a couple of games of cricket.

After ten days, I report back to Lyneham for the flight back to Changi, and am amazed to find Ginny checking in with me. She has made an impromptu trip home for a week and is on the same flight back. She doesn't say whether or not she arranged it so as to be with me and I don't ask. We're the only two passengers on a slow turboprop Britannia, and have the aircraft cabin to ourselves.

Back in the Far East in the middle of June, we found that more peace talks were under way, in Tokyo. But these too broke down almost as soon as they started, and President Sukarno publicly vowed to 'crush Malaysia by the end of the year'. The conflict in Borneo entered a new phase with increasing numbers of Indonesian regulars involved. The 1st Battalion 6th Gurkha Rifles suffered a severe reversal at Rasau in Sarawak – five killed and five wounded – in what was a professional attack. In the second fortnight of the month, the Gurkhas fought a running battle with the hundred-strong forces of a determined and persistent Indonesian commander near Kabu. Up in the hills above Pensiangan, Kabu was on the western edge of a forty-mile unmapped stretch of the border known to the soldiers as 'The Gap'.

These actions marked a new phase in the Borneo operations. As the enemy was now more organised, British infantry companies were ordered to operate from their permanent, heavily defended bases or forts with full artillery and air support. The four-man patrols stayed on the border, gathering intelligence, and incursions were met with massive retaliation, whistled up by helicopter. During July there were thirty-four attacks by Indonesian regulars, but they suffered badly, with minimal casualties among the defenders.

In all this, the transport squadrons were working round the clock and 215 Squadron Argosies were flogged almost to death. At one time just seven aircraft remained serviceable and the crews were called to fly them at all times of the day and night.

Word came that an SAS patrol had been missing for five days. A Shackleton, taking off from Labuan at dawn with an SAS operator on board, finally made radio contact with the men, still uncertain of their position. By midday the aircraft found the patrol and guided in an airdrop, but the men couldn't retrieve the supplies. Indonesians had ambushed the DZ and the SAS had no choice but to beat a hasty retreat as they'd run out of ammunition. The Shack guided in a second drop of supplies and bullets and, able to defend themselves once again, the men cleared enough jungle for the helicopters to get in and lift the men to safety.

We flew such air-support missions continuously, as did the other squadrons. We were proud to get a signal from HQ FEAF, congratulating us on: '. . . a splendid flying achievement enabling 215 to take its place alongside the more experienced squadrons.'

Not bad after ten months' action, but we didn't get too full of ourselves. After our survival experience, short as it was, we had some idea of how tough it was for the blokes down there – clothes disintegrating within a week, wet, cold and lonely at night, bitten to pieces – and shot at into the bargain.

CHAPTER SEVEN

Threat to Kuching

On 10 June 1964 the RAF base at Kuching was on high alert. Not because of any threatened attack, but because the Shadow Defence Minister, Denis Healey MP, was paying a visit. What he found was an establishment of over 500 personnel, most now on one-year unaccompanied postings. There was a detachment of three Valettas of 52 Squadron from RAF Butterworth in north Malaya and a Hastings from Changi, each flying fifty missions a month, dropping harness packs. There were dozens of helicopters, together with Single and Twin Pioneers and Army Air Corps Austers. The base was defended from air attack by a battery of Royal Artillery 40-mm radar-controlled light anti-aircraft guns, and six Javelin fighters.

RAF fighters became increasingly active. In November the year before, there had been nine Indonesian Air Force incursions into Malaysian airspace. Four were B25 Mitchell bombers escorted by P51 Mustangs. Then, on 2 February an Indonesian Tu16 Badger bomber flew at 1,000 feet over Labuan, Brunei and Sabah, followed by another later in the month. This led to an Air Defence Identification Zone (ADIZ) being set up around Sabah and Sarawak and out to 3 miles offshore. The ADIZ was enforced by four Hunters of 20 Squadron in Labuan and four in Kuching, together with two 60 Squadron Javelins in each.

Although Borneo, 800 miles north to south, was a huge area for the fighters to patrol, they mounted regular sweeps and maintained constant readiness to scramble at fifteen minutes' notice to intercept bandits. But inevitably, by the time the troops on the ground had radioed in, and the fighters had got there, the birds had flown. Targets for air-to-ground attack were scarce. Few Indonesian ground force concentrations, supply or ammunition depots, and no airfields, were to be found in the dense jungle of the frontier. Nevertheless, the fighters constantly made low-level passes to deter insurgents and to boost the morale of our guys and the locals. In times of heightened tension, they also escorted the transports on supply-drops.

These, for the Argosies of 215 Squadron, re-started at the beginning of June – from Kuching. They were tasked with ninety hours a month in support of the Western Brigade in Sarawak, and after three months, the squadron was to alternate monthly with the Hastings.

The Hastings of 48 Squadron had been on detachment at Kuching since July 1963, flying to some fourteen DZs, at the limits of their performance. Built by Handley Page at the end of the Second World War specifically as a troop transport, the Hastings saw service in the Berlin Airlift. It had a tail-wheel, for at the time of its design there was still a requirement to tow infantry-carrying gliders, and this gave the aircraft a nose-up profile on the ground. This, together with its four powerful Bristol Hercules radial engines and big props, made it a bitch to handle on take-off, and even more of one on landing. At the OCU on Thorney Island the summer before, we had watched with awe as time and again, a Hastings sashayed sideways in a ground loop on landing. While waiting at the runway crossing lights, with a Hastings coming in to land, we kept our cars ready in reverse.

The steep cabin slope made it hard work for the Army to load supplies, and pallet size was limited as everything had to go through the side doors. Loads were restricted to SEAC packs – dispatched either one at a time or all at once on an arrangement of rollers and rails – and free-fall sacks. As the dropping height was 500 feet for the packs and 50 feet for the sacks, the Hastings was unable to drop out of Labuan into the mountains. The intrepid crews tried, but found that the mountains had a greater rate of climb than did their aircraft, and many was the 'split-arse' turn, just in time, to get them out of a dead-end valley.

In the less mountainous country around Kuching, they were the kings of the harness pack drop, delivering everything from ammunition to live chickens for the Gurkhas. However, the Argosies with their 1-ton containers were brought in to bump up the supply of helicopter fuel to the Sarawak DZs. The threat to Kuching – so close to the border and the Indonesians' greatest concentration of bases – was mounting.

I'm detailed for Kuching detachment on 16 July. The crewing system means that we co-pilots get a new captain every six months or so. I'm lucky in the lottery and draw a chunky, stalwart Scotsman, Andy Adams, who knows how to bolster a rookie's fragile confidence. Our unflappable navigator is Pete Verdon, an East African hand who once coaxed a VW Beetle all the way up Kilimanjaro.

Our bags are packed for a two-week stint. Previous crews have been billeted downtown in the Borneo Hotel – single rooms with air-con and all expenses paid. But we arrive just as the new aircrew accommodation on the Station comes into service – timber huts with a separate shower block, and an open-sided mess hut nearby. I've got a room with a short unsprung bed, cabinet, chest of drawers and ceiling fan – not luxurious but all my own. We stow our kit and get down to Ops for briefing.

There's been a good deal of building since we first came here last year – the airmen are now in *basha* huts and the 215 groundcrew Whirlwind box is now an unlikely Station Armoury. There are sick quarters on the base, and the Ops Room has moved into a slightly less stifling wooden shed. The Station Cinema is now two huts with facing open ends and a screen stretched between them. Twice as many can now see the film but one half has the picture reversed – a challenge when it comes to sub-titles. In the cafeteria you can now buy two English-language news sheets, the *Sarawak Tribune* and the *Borneo Bulletin*, and keep up with all the propaganda warfare.

Just a month ago the Semengo Defence Area was set up around the base and the RAF Police were relieved by a much stronger force of the Singapore Guard Regiment, 1st Greenjackets and the Heavy Troop of the Queen's Royals. This is heartening information.

We read the safety posters, including instructions for the Duty Defence Flight, which we're all expected to know.

Issue challenge: *Berhenti! Halt – who goes there?*
Instruct: *Advance (one) and be recognised.*
On recognition: *Pass friend.*
If in doubt, cock weapon and instruct: *Stand fast – I am ready to fire.*
Use minimum force necessary at all times.

Although we're not issued with weapons, we certainly get the point. What we are issued with are Escape and Evasion kits, including a 2-foot-square map of Borneo, beautifully printed on parachute silk, showing masses of detail, but on the Indonesian side of the border only – an ominous sign. A phrasebook introduces us to some basic Malay, the lingua franca of the tribesmen. *Awas!* – Watch out! – might be useful, as would *makanan* and *minuman* – food and drink. If it came to it we wouldn't mind sampling the *borak* – rice wine – but might have a problem with the *jarit*, a Murut delicacy of pork, salt and rice, evidently buried in a split bamboo cane for months before consumption. The bag of silver *Maria Theresa* dollars we're given would provide a goodwill offering and effective bribe. This old Dutch money is apparently welcomed as currency among the natives over in Kalimantan. So, we are told, are the British sovereigns paid out as bounty in the last war and still in circulation – the gold is popular for capping teeth.

I say hello to my old Cranwell mate, Barry Priest, co-pilot on the Hastings shuttle. In the 48 Squadron Ops he shows me a small box containing three Indonesian bullets.

'Where did you find those, then?'

'Dug out of a Hastings airframe last week.'

This makes me wonder where I can find a spare flak-jacket.

On one of the doors, a notice reads ARGO and as a sub-title, Argosy Re-supply Ground Organisation. This must be us. Here, we meet the crew we're relieving as they land from their morning mission. They show us a briefing book of DZ information that's been put together, with maps, local features, safety heights and aiming points. But there's no substitute for seeing it all from the flight deck, so after tea and egg butties in the Indian cafeteria, we go along on the afternoon sortie.

My captain takes the co-pilot's seat and I stow myself in the freight compartment with the outgoing co-pilot, Brian Nicolle (known to his mates as 'Brawn'), to see, for the first time, the action down here. The soldiers have loaded the Argosy with a mixed collection of 1-ton containers and harness packs, for delivery around the nearer frontier DZs. The floors of the aircraft are taking a beating from all these heavy and sharp-edged loads. To protect them, the fitters have fixed up an emergency, but effective, set of plywood floor panels.

Brawn tells me, 'The Army's got one hell of a job getting it all in the right order. Last week there was a right cock-up – the Jocks got the rice and the Gurkhas got the bloody beer. They got on the radio and gave us a right bollocking. It was that Black Watch Major – you know, the bloke with the bagpipes in Djakarta.'

The first two 1-ton containers in the load today are ammunition for the fort at Stass, right on the border in Red Sector, just 20 miles south-west from Kuching. We get there in ten minutes, flying all the way at 1,000 feet. The dispatchers gear up for action and the clam-shell doors open. The noise is terrific, with engines and slipstream roaring like an express train. Out hurtles the container, slap goes the 'chute and the whole lot disappears down to the clearing below. Downwind, through the side window we can see that the DZ is very tight, and the load seems to have fallen between the gun and sandbags – it couldn't be closer than that.

The next container falls safely and we press on to Serikin, over hills 5 miles to the south, with two more containers of howitzer shells. Brawn points out a rocky peak standing out from the jungle, like a man's fist.

'That's Bukit Knuckle,' he shouts above the racket. 'Right on the border.'

I note that for future reference, and we continue to hug the frontier as we make for the Three Peaks DZs.

Again his pointing finger. 'See those streaks of yellow earth? Indo anti-aircraft gun positions. Don't worry – they won't fire. Don't want our guys lobbing howitzer shells down on 'em!' I want to believe him.

Along the Three Peaks ridge the DZs have code numbers: Red 336, Red 345 and so on. All the harness packs go out at 500 feet, and manoeuvring through 45- and 60-degree turns is completely disorientating down here. For the dispatchers, there's a danger, as we wheel round and round, of getting a bit nonchalant about it. The AQM is perched right out in the side doorway, looking straight down over the edge. A sudden lurch and he could be pitched off. He's got a safety line, but he'd be smashed around in the slipstream.

Then something does go wrong. The soldiers are chucking out corrugated metal roofing panels lashed to a timber base. One of them breaks up as it hits the slipstream and a panel flies up and hits a tail-boom. There's a loud crack and the aircraft shudders and bumps. It's a nasty shock for everyone, but all seems well. Up here, that is. The poor blighters down in the clearing are being bombarded with heavy iron panels, zig-zagging down like playing cards in the wind.

On the way back, the weather starts to close in. It's the summer monsoon season and an afternoon storm is drifting down to Kuching on the easterly wind. Over the intercom, we hear the captain requesting a straight-in approach – which he gets. It's touch and go, but we make it before the storm hits. We can't avoid a soaking though, running from the aircraft to the shelter of Ops, and another cup of tea.

The Ops Officer tells us, 'A signal's come in from your last DZ. They want you to know they've got enough on their plates with the Indos, without friendly fire from you lot and your roofing panels. And just in case anyone's worried, there weren't any casualties.'

The groundcrew hammers out the dent in the tail-boom and we're all set for our first mission tomorrow.

In the evening, the outgoing crew wants to show us downtown Kuching. We take a couple of beaten-up Morris Oxford taxis along a newly metalled road, past native huts standing among palms, frangipani and scrub. In the taxis' headlights we can see children clustered around cooking fires, their teeth and eyes shining in their smiling faces. The odd pig scuttles out of the way as we roll past. Nearer the town there are street lights, and the buildings are more substantial, with verandahs and pitched, wood-tiled roofs. In the town centre are concrete and stone-built shops, government buildings and porticoed villas. Beside a park is an imposing pile that we're told is the Sarawak Museum – certainly worth a visit sometime.

A block from the Sarawak River is a street market, packed now with eating stalls. This'll do for us. The dish of the day – every day – is *hum*, winkles marinated in soy sauce. They go down well, and are followed by crab. The deal is that you choose from two or three sitting in a bucket of water. The Chinese cook slaughters it before your eyes with a knife in the soft spot in its shell, plunges it into boiling water and within minutes presents the freshest crab ever tasted. Flounder is next, in sweet and sour sauce, with noodles – and Tiger beer.

We walk it off along the embankment. The river's about 200 yards wide here, in full flood, and muddy, stirred up by the monsoon rains. The lights of the Governor's Residence, the Astana Palace, shine out across the river from the other side. We're badgered by boatmen wanting to take us over, but we reckon that can wait for another day – we've got an early call in the morning.

'Good grief, what the hell do they feed their chickens on?'

No one knows, or really wants to know, as we get stuck into our poached eggs on toast. The taste is unique – pungent and unforgettable.

After breakfast, we're down at Ops by 0730 and ready to go. We're tasked with three sorties to the Red Zone DZs and the timing needs some thought. The weather in the summer Monsoon is stratus cloud in the morning and storms in the afternoon. If we take off at 0830, we can get to the closer DZs at low level under the cloud, and get back to start a second trip at 1130. Then, if we're lucky we can fit in a third sortie in the late afternoon after the worst of the storms. We'll plan for that.

We say cheerio to Brawn and his crew, flying back to Changi loaded with squaddies bound for a spell of R and R with their duty-free booze and fags – Kuching's an international flight, after all.

Our AQM and the Army have been at the aircraft since 0630, piling a staggering number of harness packs into the freight bay – fifty-three of them, totalling more than 17,000 lb. We're to drop them at three DZs – Stass and Serikin again, but first, a new one with just the code number Red 231.

There's more for me to prepare this time. The DZ controllers now have radios and I'll be able to talk to them from the air. I note down the known locations of Indonesian anti-aircraft sites and study the maps – the skipper wants me to be his second pair of eyes on the way to and over the drops.

Since I last sat up in the flight deck at Kuching, the dispersal's been extended with an acre or so of Pierced Steel Planking (PSP). It bears our weight, but it ripples as our heavy aeroplane rocks and rolls over it. The Argosy lumbers into the air at close to its maximum all-up weight. I've not seen the country round Kuching from the cockpit before. The hills are distinctive – a couple of spiky ones just to the south make great homing landmarks – and down on the border there'll be Bukit Knuckle. I can see pepper plantations – rows of conical dark-green trees. Also, the rivers can't be missed. I've marked today's flight tracks on my chart and reading from ground to map, can find the way easily under the cloud. The other co-pilot has passed on a chart with contours usefully coloured in, showing the lie of the land. Red 231 lies just a couple of miles north of Bukit Knuckle and one mile from the border.

The visibility is not too bad – the smoke haze is being kept down in Kalimantan by the prevailing wind – and the flight conditions are smooth. After ten minutes, I ask Andy for clearance to call up the first DZ on the radio.

'Roger, Roger,' he replies with a grin. I grin back – I suppose I'll have to get used to this. I tune in the DZ frequency on the UHF and press the transmit button on the control column. 'Red two-three-one, this is Alpha Romeo Golf four-four-seven. Do you read?'

There is no response. We're flying low and their aerial's sure to be deep in the trees. I'll wait a bit until we're overhead – which we soon are. I call again and hear, loud and clear: 'We see you, four-four-seven – you're clear to drop. What's the delivery today? Over.'

'Twenty packs for you, two-three-one – in ten runs – all explosives. Over.'

'Roger – we're standing by.'

I imagine the army operator down below, up to his ears in ants, with his gunners short of ammo, and praying we're not going to drop packs of howitzer shells on his head.

The captain sets up a circuit parallel with the border, close against the hills rising above us to 2,000 feet. We're dropping right into the sand-bagged gun emplacement and we'll have to be on target, ten times in a row. We come in for the first run, at 500 feet. The air's still – it should be a doddle.

The navigator from the nose, talks us in. 'Left – left – steady – red light on.' After five seconds, 'Green light on!'

The dispatchers heave a harness pack out of each side door, the 'chutes crack open and the first of twenty deliveries drifts down – well short of the target. The AQM, leaning boldly out into the slipstream calls the result.

'Fifty yards at six o'clock, Skipper.' The DZ comes on the air: 'That won't do, four-four-seven. We're not going to get that lot back, it's way outside the wire!'

Of course, there has to be a lot of defensive wire round these DZs. That concentrates the mind. What happened here? Were we too low, or did the nav have a problem with ground measurement over the trees?

'Sorry, Skipper – but at least I've got a marker now.'

He certainly has. We come round again at the same height, and the two white 'chutes hanging in the treetops give Pete a 50-yard datum from the target. The next two packs, and all the rest, drop neatly on the spot. We achieve 90 per cent accuracy – not bad for our first time out.

I say goodbye to the DZ operator, who thanks us for our efforts. We don't hang around – our dozen circuits have taken an hour and we've two DZs still to go. But the cloud's lifted, we've the best of the weather, and Serikin and Stass are close.

Yesterday, the captain and the nav saw them both, so they're quickly found and only two more packs go astray. It's 1100 already and we're not going to make an 1130 take-off for the next mission, but there's nothing I can do about that so I concentrate on map-reading.

There's a valley from Stass pointing straight as an arrow back to Kuching, with a sizeable village called Bau as a halfway checkpoint, and a major river leading us in from there. Over to starboard there are also those two spiky hills. Down here in the west there's much more to see in the way of features than in the country east of Labuan. It's all good stuff.

The next sortie will be back to the Three Peaks, with a full load of eight 1-ton containers of fuel. The chart tells me their names are Pang Amo, Plaman Mapu and Nibong. The trip should take us about an hour and-a-half, so if the Army gets us loaded quickly we might get off and back before the bad weather.

The groundcrew gets busy with the refuelling bowser, the heroic soldiers and their officer work wonders with the fork-lift and we stoke up on bacon butties and tea. At 1215 we're back in the air.

Guided by high ground to port and starboard, I can soon see, straight ahead on the nose, Batu Rawan, looming above us at 3,000 feet. It's slap bang on the border and Pang Amo lies exactly 5 miles this side of it. The Doppler's working a treat but it's still good to be able to read from the map and report: 'DZ in sight, Skipper – five miles – straight ahead.'

'Roger – I have it. Navigator and Air Quartermaster, stand by – DZ in two minutes.'

The conditions are near-perfect for dropping 1-ton containers. Pang Amo's in relatively gentle hill country and although the border's always a worry, there's no wind and the nav's really got his eye in now. We've just dropped two right in the middle of the clearing by the fort when I hear:

'You have control, Co – you do the next two drops.'

'I have control, Skipper.'

Suddenly alert, I hand the radio log across and grasp the control column with both hands. It's shaped like a sturdy pair of buffalo horns – pulled outwards from the fascia for climbing, pushed inwards for descending, and rotated for left and right. I turn downwind, flying with the DZ over to the left about 300 yards.

I've seen where Andy made his crosswind turn – just as we get to that river. Round we go, at a constant 700 feet. The speed's below 120 knots.

'Air Quartermaster – doors open.'

'Roger, Co – doors opening.'

I adjust the trim as the clam-shell doors disturb the slipstream. With the DZ to port, I bank the Argosy and turn onto the drop-path. It takes a surprising amount of muscle to pull it round at this weight with the doors open. We're now lined up on the DZ.

'Take us in, Nav.'

'Roger, Co. Right a bit – steady – red light on. Green light on!' Out she goes, and for the first time I feel for myself that jolt through the control column and the change in trim as the 1-ton bumps over the sill, and the balance alters.

'Load gone – doors closing,' says the AQM. Then, 'Ten yards at nine o'clock.'

Well done Pete, we made it. Not a world-shaking performance, but one I'm happy with – delivering a 1-ton container of dangerous Avpin helicopter starting fuel to a jungle clearing far smaller than the limits laid down in Standard Operating Procedures. I manage the next one too, and a couple more at Plaman Mapu and Nibong. We hit the target every time. We turn for base – 50 miles and a quarter of an hour away.

Emptied of its load and with a lot of the fuel gone, the 2,500-feet hills on the way back present no problem for the Argosy. But cresting them, we can see, over a wide river estuary to starboard, rain and cloud drifting across our intended track. The monsoon has brought the afternoon bad weather in right on time and we'll have to look sharp to miss it.

The skipper opens the throttles to increase our speed and checks our Doppler position with the navigator. We now have clear, flat country between us and home.

But we've no chance of missing the bad weather. We're at 4,000 feet and ten minutes from base when the rain hits the windscreen, the cloud wraps around us and the turbulence begins. Andy's flying blind, on instruments. The nearest diversion is Brunei, 400 miles away, so we're very keen to get into Kuching. I'm told to call for a radar approach.

'Kuching approach, this is Alpha Romeo Golf four-four-seven – twenty miles from Kuching bearing one-four-zero – altitude four thousand. Request ACR7 approach.'

'Roger, four-four-seven – steer three-four-zero.'

The ACR7 radar, recently installed at Kuching, locks onto the aircraft. An operator sweating inside a small hut by the runway, sees our track and distance from touchdown, on his screen. He can't measure our altitude, but he can advise what height we should be at, every half-mile. There's a constant stream of heading instructions.

'Four-four-seven, come right five degrees and commence your descent. Come left five degrees. You are at one mile – you should be at one thousand feet. Maintain your heading ....' he instructs all the way down to the runway threshold. Nothing's visible outside through the deluge and we're truly thankful for this box of tricks.

'Undercarriage down.' There are the three welcome greens.

'Flap to landing.'

The skipper's still fixed on the instruments and I peer through the wind-shield, hoping for a sight of the airfield. The ground controller's instructions continue, his voice calm and reassuring in the pouring, roaring rain.

At the very last moment, just as we're reaching the break-off height of 500 feet, when we should open the throttles to overshoot and go round again – to God knows where – I see the airfield approach lights by the runway.

'Runway in sight, Skipper!'

Andy looks up and sees the white lights – mercifully not red, which would mean we were dangerously low.

'Runway in sight – standby for landing.'

I whistle with relief as we swoop over the threshold and land – heavily, to break through the water and avoid aquaplaning. I thank the ground controller – really meaning it. He got us down, and not a moment too soon.

The storm's a big one and we're holed up in the Ops Room for two and-a-half hours, playing cribbage, the universal game of tactical transport aircrew. The groundcrew and dispatchers work on in the rain and lightning, loading and refuelling in the hope that the weather clears in time for another drop. It does, dramatically and beautifully, when the monumental clouds sail away, leaving calm air and a brilliant blue sky behind.

We take off at 1600, to the north this time, bound for Tanjong Sipang, a headland 20 miles away at the mouth of the river Santubong. Kuching town below sparkles after the rain and we're surprised to see a golf course not a mile from the centre – worth noting should we get a day off. The Santubong points straight at the headland, rising sheer out of the river delta to nearly 3,000 feet.

There's an army post here, watching out for sea-borne Indonesian incursions – and waiting today for a dozen harness packs from us. The DZ, marked with an orange balloon, is on the beach. We fly a right-hand circuit, turning out over the deep green sea. The scene is unforgettable. I'm glad the weather relented.

The weather's not so helpful the next morning, when we're tasked with a longer sortie, to Long Jawi, over 200 miles up in the Hose Mountains, halfway to Labuan. We've got a heavy mixed load of harness packs and 1-tons, and it's going to take over an hour to get there. Thanks to the Doppler, we know where we are and can climb to 14,000 feet, above the cloud.

The Hastings have to get up there along the river Rajang, at such low altitude that photos taken from the flight deck show longhouses up on the banks, above the aircraft. But then they have to leave the river to climb into the mountains, up past Nanga Gaat, the most remote forward helicopter supply base in Borneo, and, probably, the world. On one sortie earlier this week, the cloud closed down as the land rose up. Just in time, they escaped along a valley, and had to jettison 500 gallons of fuel to land back at Kuching.

After an hour and ten minutes, when the Doppler says we're over Long Jawi, we circle and wait for a hole in the cloud.

'There's one over to starboard, Skipper, and I can see the jungle underneath. Do you think it's big enough?'

'Could be, Co. Let's go see.'

With power off, full flap, and undercarriage down for good measure, we start a max-rate descent into the unknown. Moments later, the cloud closes in again. This is too bloody dangerous. So it's undercarriage up, full emergency power, and a max-rate panic climb.

I'm absolutely terrified. I stare bug-eyed at the grey soup beyond the windshield – at any moment it could turn into the towering rock-face of a new, undiscovered peak. It very nearly does. Over the intercom comes the unruffled voice of Pete Verdon.

'Ten degrees right, Skipper.' He's seen a mountain materialise on the 'cloud and clonk' radar, and as far as I'm concerned, has saved all our lives.

We get back to Kuching, to find that the weather's been so bad around Sarawak that the Argosy shuttle from Changi failed for once to get through, despite having been in the air for nearly five hours. We refuel and try again in the afternoon. It's a bumpy ride, but there are enough gaps in the heavy cloud for us to sneak into Long Jawi.

It's already notorious with the 215 Squadron crews, being on a steep-sided river valley between two peaks over 4,000 feet – one of them most likely this morning's near miss. The DZ is on the far side of a hill, on the down-slope and almost laughably small. In both undershoot and over-shoot, and along one side, there's a rushing river.

Duffy, the first Argosy navigator to try it, put his first drop – the Gurkha rum ration – 120 yards short. The Gurkhas were not best pleased, but the parachute now makes a first-class aiming point. On the DZ map there's an instruction: *Drop on Duffy's 'chute*. There it is, still in the trees as we come in for our first run, and it works a treat.

As the load goes out and the doors are closing, it's full emergency power again and a stunning, racking turn to port over the slopes and round for the next – just like the Big Dipper.

On the penultimate drop, one ton of NAAFI stores lands right on the DZ, but on the last, one ton of fuel candles into the river. We can't take the blame for a 'chute failure, so we chalk another one up to Sod's Law, say goodbye to the DZ Controller and head happily for home. It comes as a bit of a surprise when at the debriefing, the army Captain has a quiet word.

'The Long Jawi guys have radioed in. They want a replacement for the load that ended up in the river. If anyone asks, it was the NAAFI stuff that candled. OK?'

When, after nine weeks, 215 Squadron handed over to 48 Squadron at Kuching, they had flown over 100 missions, often three in a day, totalling nearly 250 hours. At the start of its service life, the Argosy was nicknamed the 'Whistling Tit' by other transport crews, possibly envious of its navaids and other luxuries. The radome on the nose certainly justified the 'tit' and the engines undoubtedly had a pronounced whistle. But now, with its clam-shell doors and 1-ton containers, it had dramatically boosted the supply-dropping capabilities of FEAF, and the nickname was dropping out of use.

It was a real achievement to deliver 1-ton containers out of Kuching. DZs were generally much smaller than those visited from Labuan, and there were no airstrips to drop on. We delivered the goods to volleyball courts – always dangerously close to the longhouses – river banks and hill tops. At Jambu, a base for naval Wessex helicopters near to Long Jawi, a 42-gallon drum of Avtur rolled off the top of the hill and took out the radio hut. Often, thirty runs of harness packs were made in the one trip. Many packs inevitably missed the tiny DZs and the supply of expensive 'chutes began to run short.

As part of a 'chute economy drive, the Gurkhas' chickens were obliged to suffer the indignity of being free-dropped in crates from 50 feet. Not altogether surprisingly, the crates broke on landing, scattering several dozen of the poor birds over the DZs. The Army therefore decided to try dropping them without crates – with disastrous results for the frantic fowls, desperately struggling to maintain height, at an exit speed of 100 miles-per-hour.

The Army also risked free-dropping corrugated panels, barbed wire and steel spikes. Fortunately for the guys in the bunkers below, this experiment with aerial bombardment was abandoned pretty quickly – but not before the steel spikes had claimed at least one flesh wound and harpooned one cookhouse.

We had the added excitement of being escorted on some missions by the Javelins that had been brought in when an Indonesian Badger flew right over Kuching. Their crews were great blokes and they did everything possible to defend us. But they didn't have the range to stay with us for long, despite the extra fuel tanks fitted for the purpose. They couldn't fly slowly enough to maintain their station on the Argosy and were always somewhere near the point of the stall. However, armed with powerful Aden cannon, interchangeable with twin Firestreak missiles, they certainly gave a feeling of greater security. On one run, south-west of Kuching, it was the Javelin that was hit by ground-fire.

One chased off an Indonesian Hercules, way off course, supply-dropping on the Malaysian side of the border. Another peeled away to speed to the scene of an Indonesian incursion on a border village. Not a shot was fired from the Javelin, but it scared off the insurgents by roaring repeatedly over the rooftops, switching its engine reheat on and off. This sounded like heavy missile launchers to the Indonesians below, who scattered.

Once, to put on a show, Boss Leary, in an Argosy up at Long Jawi, climbed to 20,000 feet. After calling for re-entry to Kuching airspace, he began a mammoth descent. He joined up with a Javelin, and at 100 feet and 265 knots – the Javelin with everything hanging to stay with it – they beat up the airfield together, with a run-in and break.

No one got a game of golf, but most of us used our few hours off to visit the longhouse at Kampong Sigu Benut, 21 miles down the Penrissen Road. This was a rare chance to see one of these fantastic structures up close. It was a marvel of engineering in bamboo and other jungle timber, held together by twisted rattan creeper, supported on stilts above the snakes and the floods. It was also above the pigs who snorted and foraged below. To get in we had to scale a steeply inclined notched pole, and were led by the Chief's son along the wide central walkway. Each family had its own living area, with cooking fire, rice jar and sleeping mats – all under a pitched *atap* (palm-leaf thatch) roof, stretching at least 50 yards and bedecked with orchids, oleander and ferns.

It was fascinating to meet the Ibans. We were in Borneo to protect their freedom, and in return they had to suffer our big feet tramping all over their private world. The way it seemed to work was this. The children played among the pigs and the old women kept an eye on them while they did the washing and cooking. The younger women and girls tended the crops (rice and vegetables) and the younger men went out hunting. No longer, we understood, for heads, but for bats, birds and monkeys. The old men sat around, smoking, chewing betel nut, and putting the world to rights.

We gave sweets to the engaging little children, who swarmed round our knees, fascinated by the hairiness of our European legs. We admired the women, as well as the Chief's collection of shrunken heads in the round-house. The winning of hearts and minds was definitely mutual.

This first detachment at Kuching improved my professional confidence no end. The photoreconnaissance work of the Canberras from Tengah was beginning to improve the quality of the charts we used. However, the mountains were often higher than indicated, and pilot navigation was still essential. We had peaks, ridges, rocks and caves to work on, as well as rivers, villages, and even individual clumps of trees – all features for the mental map.

We co-pilots were developing into useful members of the airdrop crew, with a full share of DZ runs, take-offs and landings in all weathers. In flying terms, we were coming of age.

CHAPTER EIGHT

Strife in Singapore

On our return from Kuching all hell was let loose in Singapore. On 21 July, the Prophet Mohammed's birthday, a Muslim religious procession was attacked by a Chinese mob. Hindus somehow got in on the act and the three communities went at it hammer and tongs for four or five days, fighting in the streets, and wrecking and burning cars, houses and shops. An island-wide curfew was imposed and just about all public services ground to a halt. Those who lived on Changi base were not allowed to leave and those who lived off the Station travelled on RAF buses with armed guards. On and off the base, all transport had armed guards after dark. All security measures were taken seriously. In the rioting, over a thousand locals were arrested, about five hundred were injured – and eighteen died.

Trouble had been brewing for some while. On the evening of 31 May, a small bomb went off at Changi, in the Aircraft Washing Plant (AWP). The alleged culprit, a Chinese man, was captured, as was his chief. The newspapers said that they were Indonesian sympathisers, but it was difficult to believe that the AWP could be a strategic target and the general opinion was that it was a domestic political affair. The Malaysian government was heavily biased in favour of the Malays and in Singapore this led to resentment from the Chinese, the party of power there.

The religions had mostly seemed to live together in surprising harmony. There had been a long weekend holiday in January when Chinese New Year coincided with *Hari Raya*, the start of the Muslim month of *Ramadan*. There were wild Chinese parties in Changi Village when enormous clusters of firecrackers were let off to frighten the devils away. Driving through the next morning for an early take-off, the whole place was ankle-deep in red paper from exploded crackers. Amidst the mayhem, the Muslims quietly got on with their fasting.

The Hindu festival of *Thaipusam* came later in the month. This was something we had to see. In a temple in Singapore town, devotees of the Lord Subramanyam, in a trance of ecstasy, had their supporters pierce their tongue, lips and cheeks with skewers. Evidently they felt no pain.

Dozens of rods, which looked like sharpened bicycle spokes, were then hooked into their torsos, to carry a *kavadi*, a small but weighty shrine. Strangely, no blood flowed and with much singing, chanting and incense, these believers paraded from temple to temple along the streets of Singapore. Coconuts were broken on the ground, token succour for the faithful. For a while we took photos, but feeling like intruders, we slipped away to the Raffles Hotel for a freshener. Again, such bizarrely different rites caused not a ripple of reaction from those of other beliefs.

But by the summer, political divides widened to breaking point and the race riots took off. Some of us aircrew officers were ordered to 26 Field Squadron, RAF Regiment, for riot control duties, where we met again the Smith & Wesson pistols that had weighed us down in the jungle. In practice, on the firing range we could seldom get within a yard of the target. The pistol, as many an infantry officer has found, conveys authority in a cowboy kind of way but except at very close range is really the most useless of firearms.

We were taught how to lead an anti-riot patrol of reluctant NCOs and Aircraftmen, respectively toting Sten guns and .303 rifles with bayonets. The idea was that our well-drilled and disciplined appearance would strike fear into the hearts of the racial rabble and bring order back to the streets. To our surprise, it seemed to work. We were told to pick out a ringleader and disable him by 'shooting low to maim' with the trusty pistol. Happily, none of us had to do that. Down in 'Hand Grenade Alley', as it became known, facing a hot-blooded mob yelling *Merdeka!* – Freedom! – we found that our 3-ton trucks and our military manner – but mostly the bayonets and Sten guns – persuaded the rioters to find softer targets elsewhere.

Pat did a stint as Officer of the Guard at the Station gates, and won fame for having a whole milk float unloaded, searching for bombs. There were none. His expectations deflated, he helped the hapless milkman to re-load every bottle.

For his safety, the Prime Minister of Singapore, Lee Kwan Yew, was given refuge in the government bungalow at Changi. There were mutterings from the golfers on the station nine-hole course when his notoriously slow game held up play, and his security entourage trampled the greens.

Through it all we continued to get on famously with the Chinese civilian staff. Our batmen still waited on us hand and foot, with a smile. Taff Howell had a hiring in Katong, outside Changi. A ten-strong Chinese family lived next door and because of this the RAF Police insisted the Howells shelter at Katong police station.

'Not a chance, Jimmy!' Jeannie, Taff's doughty young Glaswegian wife, sent them packing and promptly accepted their Chinese neighbours' friendly invitation to move in with them. They came to no harm.

The Hastings of 48 Sqn dropped 200lb harness packs out of Kuching for four arduous years. *(Crown Copyright)*

Batu Lawi – the Witch's Tit – the most reliable of landmarks. *(Courtesy J.M. Leary)*

The soldiers of the RASC toil to load 1-ton containers onto the Argosy at Labuan.
(Crown Copyright)

and bravely push them out over Borneo. *(Crown Copyright)*

The navigator searches for the DZ.
(Crown Copyright)

First 1-ton delivery on the way...
(Crown Copyright)

...nearly there...

...coming round with more...   *(Crown Copyright)*

...and a low level salute to finish. *(Crown Copyright)*

The author at RAF Changi with Riley and Argosies. *(Courtesy I. Simons)*

Dorothy Allen and pupils at Changi Junior School. *(Courtesy Mrs B. Priest)*

Malay Kampong and communal well.

Bullock Carts outside Malacca.

215 Sqn aircraftmen carolling for charity, and Tiger Beer, in the Officers' Mess at Christmas.
(Courtesy M. Robson)

FEAF Jungle Survival Course. *(Courtesy B. Priest)*

45 Sqn Canberras over Mount Kinabalu. *(Crown Copyright)*

20 Sqn Hunters over Pulau Tioman. *(Crown Copyright)*

Just beating the storm – Argosy returning to Kuching dispersal. *(Courtesy M. Robson)*

Bario landing strip and DZ on the Plain of Bah. *(Crown Copyright)*

Kubaan DZ.

Rumah Lusong DZ. *(Crown Copyright)*

Lio Matu DZ with pepper plantation navaids. *(Crown Copyright)*

The dreaded Pensiangan looking upstream. *(Courtesy R. Twitchett)*

One in the middle at Pensiangan. *(Courtesy R. Twitchett)*

Wall of rock, Milford Sound NZ.   *(Courtesy T.J. Sneddon)*

RNZAF Bristol Freighter over a *kelong* off Changi Point.

The Astana, over the Kuching river. *(Courtesy J.M. Leary)*

Dyak greeting party for the aircrew visitors. *(Courtesy J.M. Leary)*

Changi Splash – author below, padre above.

Inside a Sarawak longhouse.

Art Smith navigates round his coffee cup. (*Courtesy R.A. Miller*)

215 Sqn personnel at Changi 1965. (*Crown Copyright*)

After a couple of weeks the Malayan leader, the Tunku up in Kuala Lumpur, promised more representation for the Chinese in government and by the end of the month the curfew was lifted. The riot control worked so well that the Station Commander established a permanent Armed Service Reserve, as part of an overall Passive Defence Plan.

I'm pleased to have had this riot-control experience when, a couple of weeks later, my number comes up and I'm Station Orderly Officer for the day. I'm somewhat nervous. This is the RAF's biggest station, and I'm a mere twenty-four-year-old Flying Officer. To the tough nuts in the Other Ranks, and in the army barracks, I'm hardly out of the cradle, but I get away with striding through the Sergeants' and Airmen's Messes, intoning at every table: 'Orderly Officer – any complaints?' – and smiling thinly at the caustic responses.

One of the airmen at dinner, 'Wee Jimmy MacKenna from Fife', is well-known to me. A small, wiry Scotsman and champion flyweight boxer, Jimmy was, although a tireless worker, perpetually in trouble, usually when he 'had a drop taken'. There was the time when he launched a barrage of frozen chickens at the CO at the Squadron party. And he would regularly pit his 5 ft 6 in and 8 st frame against the largest bloke in sight. This gives me pause for thought as tonight I'm the largest bloke in sight. But he knows that we're both good friends of Horse, who more than once has bailed him out of the Guardroom. So it seems I'm off his hit list.

At the Guardroom I manage to deal with the odd drunken squaddie – the uniform and rank flashes seem to do the trick. I'm just settling down on my camp bed for a quiet smoke and perhaps a doze, when the phone rings frantically in the outer office. The Orderly Sergeant comes to get me.

'Trouble in the barracks, Sir. The Land Rover's waiting.'

Stationed in the Selarang barracks at Changi are the Argyle and Sutherland Highlanders, known to enemy and friend alike as the 'Poisoned Dwarfs'. They've done great things in Borneo and are back for a bit of R and R. One big fellow's taken a few drams down at the NAAFI Club and has come home to have it out with his missus. He wants to know what she's been doing while he's been away – and who with. He's barricaded them both in their quarter and the racket is bringing the block down. Fearful for the girl's safety, a neighbour has phoned the Guardroom. I'm duty-bound to sort it out – armed only with the Orderly Officer's white armband. I have a brainwave and take the burly Orderly Sergeant in with me. He's married, and understands these things. So much so that after a while, both man and missus are crying on our shoulders – and we put the kettle on.

Away from the squadrons we bachelors didn't mix that much with our married colleagues, and even less with their families. The Wednesday night Amahs' Market and the evening films were where we were most likely to bump into them, but we formed two largely separate groups. They had the Married Families' Club with cafeteria, beer-bar and weekly dances and social evenings. The offspring had Girl Guides and Brownies, Scouts and Cubs, and Sea Rangers. Married officers lived in quarters and hirings dispersed around and outside the station and came to Temple Hill, perhaps for major events but not much to the bar, the social centre for most of the bachelors.

Some families did invite us to their houses. The 215 Squadron Commander and his young wife, Diana, hosted receptions at their quarter. At one particular hiring in a nearby *kampong* there was always a welcome. The husband, who was away a lot on twelve-hour patrols in the Shackletons, appeared to be willing to loan his house, beach and boat for water-skiing parties some Sundays – and his missus mixed exotic cocktails in the Kenwood Chef. Horse and his wife, Jill, laid on regular darts afternoons when we picked up curry and rice in banana leaves from Changi Village, and they generously supplied the chilled Tiger beer. Then at Christmas, many a family kindly risked having us bachelors at the festive table.

Two of the group of Cranwell graduates joined the married community while in Singapore, both of them co-pilots on 48 Squadron. Johnny Fittus had a high-profile wedding, making the front page of the *Straits Times.* The bride, a pert young Pan Am stewardess, arrived for the ceremony straight off her Boeing. The airline's gift (with an eye to a good publicity angle) was the one night stop-over honeymoon in the penthouse suite of the Hotel Singapura – the love-nest festooned with orchids. The other, Barry Priest, met Dorothy Allen, a charming ex-pat teacher from the junior school and asked her to the Tuesday film at the Officers' Club. It wasn't long before he proposed over a candle-lit dinner at the Casuarinas Hotel – and the date was set. Because he was under twenty-five he had to ask the Station Commander's permission and could expect no married allowance. They had to get themselves home to England for the wedding, and on their return, Dorothy lost half her overseas allowances. With hurdles like that, not many entered the marriage stakes, love conquering all.

There was more trouble in Singapore and Malaya at the end of August. Malaysia Day came around and Indonesian insurgents – the *Straits Times* said there had been a number of landings in past weeks – stirred up the left-leaning, and therefore Indo-inclined, Chinese. Guards were doubled at Changi and three RAAF Sabrejets flew down from Butterworth to strengthen air defences.

The next day a thousand armed Indonesian regulars landed by sea at Pontian, just up from Johore Bahru on the west coast of Malaya, and a few days after that, ninety-six Indonesian paratroopers dropped from a C-130 at Labis, inland from Malacca. At the same time, an Indonesian flotilla bombarded an Esso bunkering station off Singapore, as well as the Malaysian patrol craft that came to its defence. These attacks were ineffectual, but the paratroopers were not mopped up till the end of October.

The riots and landings prompted the Malaysian government to declare a State of Emergency on 3 September. The Argosies of 215 Squadron were dispersed to other airfields, vital Changi buildings were sandbagged and slit trenches dug. Local civilians were kept off the base, guns were deployed and all leave was cancelled. More Sabrejet fighters arrived from Butterworth and six more Shackletons flew in from Ballykelly in Northern Ireland, together with naval Buccaneer fighter-bombers off HMS *Victorious*.

On 9 September the Tunku appealed to the UN Security Council, and a resolution was moved requiring Indonesia to end its aggression. This was vetoed by the Soviets. After close on two years of Confrontation, Britain's resolve was still strong, but her resources were becoming stretched. Assistance was needed.

The Australian and New Zealand governments were becoming increasingly concerned at the aggression of their massive next-door neighbour and British diplomacy set out to win their support. As part of that effort, eighteen senior officers from the UK Imperial Defence College (IDC) were sent on a month-long tour of Australasia. The Argosy was detailed to carry them and it was my good luck to be selected as co-pilot. My usual captain, Andy Adams, was the skipper and Tom, the navigator. He was the only navigator on the squadron qualified at the time to carry VIPs, and he'd flown the tortuous route to Australia via Cocos Island, avoiding Indonesia, just the month before.

When we picked up the distinguished party at Cunderdin airfield outside Perth in Western Australia, they turned out to be a jovial bunch from all three services, led by a full Admiral. They bowled up late, greatly amused by a brush they'd had with the law. An Aussie traffic cop, singularly unimpressed by a bus-load of high-ranking military Poms, had taken his time booking their driver for speeding. We were glad to have made it ourselves, having hit the mother and father of all storms on the night sector between Port Hedland and Perth. We met rain, hail, lightning and turbulence, and lumps of ice, flying off the propellers, had peppered the fuselage, leaving a dotted line of dents up both sides.

Our first stop was the vast artillery and rocket-testing range at Woomera. While the brass hats were shown the sights, Tom and I organised our own tour, bumming a ride in a Bell helicopter. With nothing for hundreds of miles in any direction and not much after that, we skimmed over the desert at zero feet, closing in on big buck kangaroos that did their best to aim kicks at the hovering machine.

As we progressed eastward over the Great Australian Fanny Adams, my attempts to make radio contact with such places as Meekatharra, Ooldea, Tarcoola and Kingoonya provided a number of mirthful moments for both the guys on the ground and those on the flight deck. Calling in to Wagga Wagga – pronouncing it as written – I met, not for the first time, the masterly Australian combination of pity and scorn.

'It's *Woggah Woggah,* mate!'

In New Zealand, as a respite from their high-level negotiations, browsing and sluicing, we took our VIPs on a tour of the scenic wonders of Mount Cook and Milford Sound. At 8,500 feet we slalomed in and out of the snow-clad mountains and circled the peak, the glaciers flashing underneath us. Our passengers, like schoolboys on a day trip, careered around the freight bay, cameras in hand. The flight deck offered an even better view and I was turfed out of my seat to make way for the Admiral, who sat there in dignified splendour. No one had the heart to tell him he had the head-set on the wrong way round, with the microphone at the back of his neck.

Milford Sound is a winding fjord, half-a-mile wide and 9 miles long with sheer walls dropping from a snowy 900 feet on both sides to water level and then another 1,300 feet below that. Flying up it at 500 feet was no problem, but what we met at the top – a wall of solid rock – presented a terrifying dead-end. We just had to turn back. The Argosy isn't built for aerobatics but the skipper managed a turn steep enough to be classified as a wing-over. By the skin of our teeth, we were pointing back down the fjord but immediately facing another dilemma. Which of the necessary turns would bring us out over the open sea, and which would have us confronting sheer cliffs again? Inspired, Tom chose the right one and some of Britain's finest military minds, engrossed in their lenses and camera angles, never knew how close they'd come to meeting a watery end at the bottom of the world.

Our take-off from Christchurch was at an ungodly hour, oh-dark-thirty according to Tom, and when, many gale-buffeted hours later and well behind schedule, we landed at Mount Isa in Western Queensland, we were thirsty. Mount Isa had the reputation of being a rugged mining town full of rugged mining types.

All round Australia it had been: 'Wait till you get to Mount Isa, mate – then you'll see how Aussies can drink.'

This was something our crew hadn't had much chance to do on the tour so far. On the first night-stop, on the glorious coral island of Cocos, we were told by one of the colourful gang of Qantas stewards who ran the hotel, that the beer had run out.

'Boat don't arrive before next week, mate. You should've been here last week.'

We'd had 'beer from the pipe' at RAAF Pearce and at RNZAF Whenuapai, near Auckland, where, after closing time, a flexible hose was fed through the bar grille in order to satisfy demanding thirsts. But the 'six o'clock swill' was a feature of Aussie life and we'd fallen foul of it on several occasions. Here at Mount Isa we were expecting great things.

But we were too late. The bar was closed. We left at 1100 the next day before it opened.

While our charges were taken off to see the official sights of Papua New Guinea, next on our route, Tom and I managed to head off into the interior in a hired Holden – either a brave or a foolish thing to do. After sheltering from torrential rain under a longhouse among the pigs and chickens, dodging the attentions of curious natives (possibly still cannibalistic?) and rescuing the Holden from sinking sand, it was a relief to get back to mundane crew routine.

We waved goodbye to our VIPs in Darwin. They were clearly delighted with the results of their vital strategic trip. Intending to get quietly tiddly in recognition of a job well done, we went into a bar and saw again the wide variety of glasses Australians like to drink from. The 'bidi' was slightly bigger than the 'midi' and the 'schooner' was, surprisingly, bigger still. There was another tankard-shaped one, even larger, which wouldn't have looked out of place hanging in an English pub.

'I'll have one of those, please. What's it called?'

Again, that pitying scorn. 'Bloody pint, mate.'

The wind was against us all the way from Darwin back to Cocos. After nearly eleven flying hours, we trailed into the hotel bar, visions of cold, golden liquid before our eyes. The steward sorrowfully shook his head.

'Should've been here last week, mate.'

On our return, 215 Squadron had been on duty (often on a sweaty trench-digging detail) and permanent standby for about twenty-five days and the Mess was crawling with strangers, many of them wearing army khaki or navy whites. One of the navy uniforms, or more to the point, the dashing

RNAS Buccaneer pilot inside it, had succeeded in sweeping my girlfriend Ginny off her feet and into his life. And that was that. Before my month away, we'd both been harbouring doubts about any long-term future and so, after a suitable period, morosely nursing pints of Tiger long into the evening, I got over it.

Reports reached us that the IDC tour was a great success socially, politically and militarily. After strong political pressure, and for reasons of enlightened regional self-interest, both Australia and New Zealand had agreed to commit forces to the Borneo struggle from the new year. Indonesian landings, attempted landings and sabotage continued through October and November, President Sukarno continuing to boast that he would crush Malaysia. But the attacks did little more than disrupt civilian life and divert the security forces from Borneo. As some kind of retaliation, RAF Hastings and Argosies, and RMAF Twin Pioneers, dropped more than three million leaflets in the dead of night on Indonesian forward bases over in Sumatra. They carried a message from a captured Indonesian paratroop officer, discrediting President Sukarno's propaganda. The raid was the first overt violation of Indonesian airspace in Confrontation.

The ADIZ was extended up to the Thailand border but the incursions didn't stop. On 23 December a 740-strong force of Indonesian regulars made a sea-borne attack in Western Malaya. Some 300 were repulsed before they landed and of the rest, 142 were killed and 300 captured. Often at night, Argosies provided airborne radio relays for the ground forces and helicopters and flew low, simulating Indonesian Hercules to flush out the insurgents. At Changi, over sundowners at the Officers' Club, we could see Malaysian Marine craft setting out from Fairy Point jetty for their regular night patrols, and the carriers *Eagle*, *Ark Royal*, and *Victorious* – even the occasional black and sinister submarine – sailing majestically up the Straits to the naval base at Sembawang. When Indonesian anti-aircraft guns started random firing from the off-shore islands – twice hitting a Hastings on approach – air-traffic patterns were hastily altered.

On Christmas Eve the Station Commander sets out on his annual inspection of section bars. There are sixteen this year, ranging from a French-style *boîte de nuit* with two WRAF *femmes méchantes* in fishnet stockings, to one with all the trappings of the Wild West including singing barbers. As he's awarding the last prize, reports come in of Indonesian sampans in the Malacca Straits. An armed Shackleton is scrambled and finds seven of them. The minesweeper HMS *Ajax* takes them in tow and hands them over to Special Branch.

On one of the Shackletons from Ballykelly it's good to see Hugh Rolfe, an old friend from Cranwell and Oakington. He's co-pilot on patrol that evening over the Malacca Straits and invites me along for the ride. It's a dramatic four hours, flying so low that to make a turn, the pilot has to gain height to keep the wing tip out of the water. As darkness falls, ships' mast-lights appear above us and we have to climb sharply to avoid them.

Close to the Indonesian coast I ask, 'See those flashing lights?'

'Those aren't lights, they're tracer shells,' says Hugh coolly.

The noise from the huge piston engines is absolutely deafening – happily only temporarily. Back at the Mess for a recovery drink, I hear that it took five days to fly out to Singapore via Aden and Gan, and the whole trip was at 1,000 feet.

Hugh tells me that the other night, they were on patrol over the Malacca Straits teamed with one of our minesweepers, both under strict orders to keep away from the Indonesian shoreline. On its radar, the Shackleton identified a vessel lurking up a river estuary. Looking for a bit of action, the skipper closed in and illuminated the ship with flares. And there in the glare – also seeking to relieve the tedium with a spot of illicit surveillance – was the minesweeper.

'And for that,' he says laconically, 'we get the GSM.'

The authorities have decided that the General Service Medal (GSM), with Borneo clasp, is to be awarded for active service in the campaign, backdated to December 1962. This leads to a spate of extra visitors on the Borneo shuttles, with staff and ground-tour people understandably keen to earn their qualifying time at the sharper end of affairs.

Another medal is awarded this Christmas. In the New Year Honours, my first captain, Boss Leary, gets the Air Force Cross (AFC). This – a very senior flying decoration indeed – is for '... meritorious service in supply-dropping in the Borneo theatre'.

In his typically modest fashion, Boss Leary says that the AFC is in recognition of the work of the whole squadron. Of course that's right – but he's earned his award and is due great respect. I feel a particular pride having been with him on many missions. On one of those certainly, and probably on more, he saved my life.

CHAPTER NINE

En Route

While the conflict in Borneo hogged most of the limelight and a large slice of the flying effort, the crews of 215 Squadron had to carry on with their other key task – route-flying on regular shuttles within the Far East theatre. By the middle of 1964, RAF boffins had fitted the Argosies with removable long-range tanks. Allegedly belly tanks off the Meteor jet, there were four of them (each 8 feet by 3 feet) mounted two each side of the freight bay towards the front. They gave the Argosy a strategic range but limited the payload space available, and the fire risk ruled out carrying passengers. However, they made it possible to fly the longer sectors necessary to reach far-flung and exotic destinations like Korea and Easter Island. We could now make it in one hop to Cocos. But the bread-and-butter runs outside the Borneo bases, where long-range tanks were not needed and we could carry passengers and freight, were to Hong Kong and Thailand.

I go to Bangkok many times – or rather to Don Muang International Airport. The problem is that the Argosy's performance is good enough to get there from Changi and back in one day, avoiding the need to night-stop. This is a frustrating situation as the flesh-pots of Bangkok are calling.

Some of the guys make it. There's a regular week-long Navigation Trainer trip around Thailand, with lodgings at the Victory Hotel in downtown Bangkok before flying off to Ubon, Udorn and on to Chieng Mai and another town centre hotel. One of each groundcrew trade goes on the aircraft, and they regale us for days afterwards in the Chalet club with sordid tales of sex and drunken violence.

In May 1964, one lucky crew – not a bachelor among them – spent twelve days stationed in Bangkok, flying troop shuttles up-country on a South East Asia Treaty Organisation (SEATO) exercise involving Thai, US and British forces. They arrived back in the squadron crew-room looking frankly knackered. They told us of a dinner hosted by the Chief of the Thai Air Force where a girl escort was provided for each visiting officer. Word is that the wives all required an energetic performance of their husbands' marital duties on the night of their return, as some dubious kind of reassurance they'd behaved themselves when away.

We unmarried men seem to have our own code, generally speaking, although our personal lives don't come in for much discussion. After some seven years without the benefit of co-education and then, for some of us, another three of military college, our experience of sex is understandably limited. It appears to involve a high degree of commitment, not least because of the potentially inconvenient results. But that's not to say we're all long on honour and short on passion. It's a confusing time, with rising hemlines leaving less and less to the imagination and women beginning to claim more and more of the initiative.

In the Borneo longhouses, so we're told, there's a different climate of opinion altogether. No commitment is expected and among the available experienced women – young widows and spirited girls – it's a matter of pride when the Chief encourages them to entertain his honoured guests and their hospitality can prove to be extremely educational. But the longhouses are inaccessible to us freighter crews so it's Bangkok, in the imagination at least, that offers the chance to throw off inhibitions once and for all.

Take-off for the Thailand shuttle is ridiculously early. The route lies due north up the Malayan peninsula and over the Gulf of Siam and we arrive in just over four hours. Bangkok airport is always busy, so much so that on at least one occasion the harassed local controller just stops talking and lets the aircraft sort themselves out. Our Argosy is refuelled by the Borneo Company, an offshoot of BOAC. Their call sign is Speedbird Bangkok, inventively rendered by one of the co-pilots as Speedcock Bangbird.

In the airport restaurant it's hard to concentrate on the grilled *plakapong*, the delicious local fish, for all the strikingly beautiful Thai girls passing by the table. I'm dragged away to continue the flight to Ubon, an hour-and-a-half east up on the Laos border. We're carrying troops, building materials, and tentage for the 'canvas Hilton' – accommodation for the Royal Engineers constructing a hush-hush fighter airfield at Mukhadan. This is close to the Laos border and is for the use, in due course, of American combat aircraft. The Yanks are forbidden by the SEATO treaty to build bases in Thailand but if the Brits take on the job of construction, then where's the problem chum?

There's a long wait at Ubon while our consignment of Royal Engineers drives from the airfield to Mukhadan and another lot drive back. The squaddies come bouncing through the dust in their 3-tonner, raring for their R and R. They clamber on board and we take off for home, five hours' direct flight south. As we climb away, the setting sun throws flares of glorious red light across a line of storm clouds over the Gulf of Siam. They stretch from horizon to horizon – right across our route. The sight has the impact of a punch in the stomach.

The sunlight catches the anvil-headed cu-nimbs while down below, over the darkening sea, white lightning flashes continuously. There's no option but to plough on. In almost black-out conditions, rain lashes the wind-screen and the airframe corkscrews in the columns of turbulent air. Water finds its way into the aeroplane, fusing forty different circuit breakers and causing three spurious engine fire warnings. Lightning takes out the CCWR, causing merry hell, and we endure an hour of switchback riding before being ejected from the storms into calmer air. Landing at Changi after midnight makes it a long day.

Chieng Mai is the destination on other occasions. Way up on Thailand's northern border with Burma, it's 1,500 feet above sea level and ringed by 8,000-feet mountains. The British Vice-Consul here entertains RAF crews lucky enough to night-stop. He's been in residence for fourteen years, and being the only officer of his grade in the Foreign Service who speaks Thai, intends to remain for another fourteen. Tom tells of a billet in a hotel in town where rooms can be hired by the hour, and a notice on the wall reads: 'Welcome 48 Squadron'. A cinema in town is showing *Cleopatra* with Richard Burton and Elizabeth Taylor dubbed in squeaky Thai – and sub-titled in Chinese. In a magnificent Buddhist temple on Sutrup Mountain, 1,500 feet above the town, cotton and silk weaving, and umbrella and paper making can all be seen. Tom buys lacquer and silver ware, wood carvings and Thai silk from a shop assistant said to have been 'Miss Thailand 1963'. He watches traditional dancing performed by 300 local girls, every one a potential 'Miss Thailand 1964'.

I get to see the airport.

There's always a night-stop in Hong Kong. The Argosies run a passenger and freight shuttle to the British colony at least once a month, allowing two days to get there and back and one for local training at the unique airfield in Hong Kong harbour – with a few hours off.

The aircrew bus arrives outside the *basha* at the ungodly hour of 0430 and collects my next-door neighbour Art, and me. Dickie Miller is our captain on this flight, and at flight-planning, he advises: 'Pay particular attention to the weather – it's a mixed bag. A lot depends on the position of the ITCZ.' I find myself wishing I'd paid more attention at those met lectures.

'You'll remember, in October this lies from Burma, across Thailand and on to the Central Philippines, right across our route.' That sounds a bit dodgy.

He continues: 'We can expect it to be cyclonic with extensive thunder.' It *is* dodgy. 'When we get there it'll be wet and cool. It's been raining since June and the tail end of the south-west monsoon is still around.'

I wonder if I'm going to enjoy this trip. After the daily 84 degrees at Changi, Hong Kong's 65 is going to seem positively arctic to our tropic-thinned blood.

'Finally,' says the skipper, 'we're told to look out for tropical storms, known out here as typhoons – there are no fewer than five roaring around the China Sea.'

We're also warned to take extra care around Saigon, where we land to refuel, as the Vietnam cauldron's beginning to come to the boil. In October 1964 there are no fewer than 23,000 US military advisers in the country, and a task force of American ships off the coast.

The first leg is straight up the east coast of Malaya to Kota Bahru. The dawn comes up over the South China Sea – 'like a sparrow's fart', as Art poetically puts it. From Kota Bahru our course for Saigon is north-east over the sea, another couple of hours' flying away. Crossing the Vietnam coast, we get a clear view of the mouths of the Mekong river – silver deltas glinting in the sun. In these greenest of jungles there's no hint of the mayhem brewing further north.

The approach to Saigon's Tan Son Nhut airport is a hair-raising experience, a case of finding a way through a mix of inter-continental jets and swarming US helicopters. At the airport terminal we're met by the RAF liaison officer, an extraordinary character, reputedly gone slightly barmy – in tune with most in Saigon just now, it seems. He has developed a bar-room trick of draining his glass, and then eating it – not exactly a comfortable idea. I concentrate on the delicate Vietnamese girls in their floating silk tunics.

We've carried passengers as far as Saigon – shadowy cloak-and-dagger types who disappear into the arms of US uniformed personnel. Replenished and refuelled, we take off, jostle with airborne traffic again, and set course for the four-and-a-half hour leg to Hong Kong.

In another hour or so, out over the sea, we cross a shoal of coral islands – North Reef. It's our turning point and we're half way. It's here that a randy 48 Squadron navigator made history by informing his Hastings crew: 'Overhead North Reef – Hong Kong dead ahead – cocks to magnetic.'

Our navigator is pretty creative too. Bored with following the interminable dead-straight track over the South China Sea, Art eyes the paper cup on his chart table and flicks on his boom-mike.

'Nav to Skipper. Come ten degrees starboard, please.' The captain complies, glad to have something to do. Ten minutes later there's a further request.

'Come twenty degrees port.'

This time, Dickie Miller asks, 'Why the hell are we weaving about the sky, Nav?'

'Just diverting round my coffee, Skip.'

An hour on from North Reef we start a cruise descent – nose down, throttles as they are, building up to maximum speed – and half-an-hour later we can see the stunning panorama of Hong Kong laid out beneath us, an amphitheatre of jewel-like islands in a blue sea, set against a backdrop of hills on the very edge of China. There's little time for sight-seeing though, as the approach and landing here is one of the most difficult in the world and demands full attention from the whole flight deck. No captain is allowed to land at Hong Kong before he's been checked in by someone who's done it before. The name of the brave man who did it for the first time remains a mystery.

Our first landfall is Cheung Chow island, strewn with hulks of ships wrecked in the typhoons. We fly across the waters to Stonecutters Island, and on to the Kowloon Peninsula, watching the mountains rising to the New Territories and the Chinese border beyond. We're at 600 feet as we pass Hong Kong Island to starboard, heading straight for the mountain-side – and for the blocks of flats that climb the hill. The captain's aiming-point is a cricket-square-sized chequer-board pattern, painted on a cliff-face above the flats. At the last possible moment he hauls the Argosy into a steep right-hand turn, all the way round over the Kowloon rooftops until we're pointing back almost to where we came from. And there, full in front of the windscreen and half-a-mile ahead, is Kai Tak airfield, with a single runway built out into the harbour. Now it's undercarriage down, then full flap, the tyres squeal on the tarmac and we've managed another successful, and semi-miraculous, landing in the British Crown colony of Hong Kong.

The Argosy is placed in the capable care of the Hong Kong Aircraft Engineering Company (HAEC). They handle all the aircraft movements here as well as refuelling, service and maintenance. They've been around a long time and give the airfield its reputation for British colonial efficiency.

The bus takes us to the RAF Officers' Mess, up on the hillside above the runway. After a three-course meal (soup, meat and two veg with pudding – no Chinese option today) Dickie, Art and I sit out on the verandah in neo-colonial splendour with our San Miguel beer, brewed in the Philippines. It's very quiet up here, high above the busy airfield.

'What's that funny noise?' I ask. 'Every few minutes – a sort of pattering sound.'

'Not raining, is it?'

'No, I've heard it before, Art. Just a minute, it's coming from those flats.' We look across at the open windows not far away, where groups of Chinese can be seen hunched over tables, engrossed in what appears to be some kind of game.

'I've got it – it's mah-jong tiles rattling!'

Over on Hong Kong Island, lights shine out from the Peak. It looks enchanted, like Bali Hai from *South Pacific* – and just as intriguing. In half-a-dozen visits here I've never made it up to the top. Perhaps tomorrow.

The next morning I get my wish. We're not flying until the afternoon and the weather's not nearly as bad as was threatened so Art and I hire a coolie and his rickshaw to take us down to the Star Ferry. This is the way to travel – convenient, ecologically friendly, and cheap. There's a particular pleasure in feeling the rumble of the wheels, and hearing no engine noise. We are rather exposed though, in the heavy Hong Kong traffic – particularly alongside the red double-decker buses (imported from London) that tower over us.

The Star Ferry is a Hong Kong landmark – or perhaps watermark? Its boats, twin-deckers with ramps at both ends, shuttle between Kowloon Pier and the Island all day and most of the night. The ten-minute ride in the sunshine over the sparkling water of the harbour is a refreshing change from the bustle of the Kowloon streets. The view's magnificent too, with the Peak rising in front – and behind us, the cliffs towering up to Lion Rock.

The ferries have to dodge through a throng of water traffic – motor launches, sampans, freighters and Chinese junks, making their stately progress under full sail. Further up the harbour, half a dozen ocean-going liners are moored.

Over on the Island, the Star Ferry terminal leads right into the Chinese shops and open-air market, close to the business quarter in Victoria town. The watch I haggled for in Singapore fell apart in Australia, and here's a chance to replace it with a better one. I pay with a Chartered Bank cheque, denominated in Singapore dollars.

'How will that cheque work here?'

'Don't know how they organise their finances, Art – but I reckon the cheque's a currency itself. One I wrote in Kowloon six months ago still hasn't been cashed.'

A funicular railway rattles us up the steep, wooded slopes on the north side of the Peak, and Hong Kong unfolds around us. Below is the crowded harbour, half-a-mile wide, and across the water, the industrial and shopping area of Kowloon, with shanty towns clinging to the cliffs above, and Lion Rock and the 3,000-feet hills of the New Territories beyond. We're told that within view live over four million people (the vast majority of them Chinese) and that China tolerates this last colonial toehold because of the value of its trade.

Up on the summit – where the Union flag and cannon symbolise British colonial might – we can see out to the encircling islands and reefs. From our vantage point we watch, fascinated, the Boeing 707s and Comets making the same approach and landing over Stonecutters Island and Kowloon that we made last night – and those taking off, snaking through the Gap, the channel out through the hills to the south. Down below, the corniche road winds round to Aberdeen harbour and its floating Chinese restaurant boats.

They make us think about lunch and we set off on foot down to Victoria town. I'm glad to have conquered the Peak but I have mixed feelings. This is where the nobs live, in their colonial-style mansions behind trim hedges enclosing manicured gardens. It somehow reminds me of Surbiton – and the Peak's no longer my enchanted Bali Hai.

In the afternoon, after an elegant cup of tea in the Mess, the bus takes us back to our aeroplane, for two hours of circuits and approaches. We practise radar patterns inside the magnificent harbour, out to Stonecutters Island and through the Gap. It's good to take advantage of the clearer October air. Old Sunderland flying-boat skippers tell us that in the worst of the monsoon cloud and rain they used to land on the sea beyond the islands and taxi in. After an hour, darkness falls and thousands of lights reflect off the water, joining the flashing neons of Kowloon. But the final approach from the chequer-board is mesmerising – from this point on, no flashing lights are allowed, save those on the airfield itself.

Before leaving the aircraft, I call Changi on the single side-band radio.

'FEAF Ops – this is Mike Oscar Kilo Oscar Golf. How do you read? Over.'

'Reading you loud and clear.' The response is immediate, and truly amazing. At night, the long-wave signals bounce off the upper layers of the atmosphere, all the way down to Singapore, nearly 1,600 miles away. I ask FEAF to tell the squadron that we plan to fly direct to Changi tomorrow, weather permitting.

Then, it's off to Nathan Road for some Chinese food, with Tsingtao beer, and on to Happy Valley for the pony races. Down among the high-rise buildings of Kowloon, trotting ponies, pulling one-man chariots with Chinese and Australian drivers, chase each other furiously round and round an oval track. I tower like Gulliver over the hordes of Chinese race-goers and they pester me to give them a high-altitude running commentary on the progress of their favourite.

With modest winnings in the pocket, it's time to go and find some girls. The Eagle's Nest nightclub on the top floor of the Hilton is a favourite hunting ground. Art tells me that once when he was there, the cabaret was the Lionel Blair Dancers, out from England and looking for a good time. The crew brought the girls back to Kai Tak Mess – where the expatriate schoolteachers were already well into the gin-slings at their own party. At the height of the action, Lionel himself arrived, in all his camp glory.

'That night,' says Art, 'was bizarre.'

Our night is quite noteworthy too, and next morning, sore in the head, lighter in the pocket, and our thoughts still full of amorous encounters, we report for flight-planning and briefing. The typhoons have blown off down into the Pacific Ocean, and we're cleared for our seven-hour one-hop return to Changi. We trundle out through the Gap, drone over North Reef, and coast into Vietnamese airspace. An inquisitive Yankee interceptor comes up off its carrier to meet us. He sees our familiar RAF roundels, waggles his wings and dives away. Hurled about by the promised thunderclouds over the Gulf of Siam, and by the duty cu-nimb over Fairy Point, we're thankful to bump down at Changi in time for dinner.

CHAPTER TEN

Labuan Revisited

In October 1964, a 215 Squadron Argosy was *en route* for Labuan, to
reactivate the supply-dropping detachment. It was fortunate to make
it. With a cabin full of Marines, it had trouble climbing out of Changi,
needing twenty minutes on emergency power – three times longer than
normal – to get away. All the instrument readings were normal so the
captain pressed on, but could only make it to just over half the normal
cruising height. The aircraft staggered along to Labuan, where, on a
hunch, the captain had the Marines weighed. They were found to be
excessively heavy, the Regimental Sergeant Major himself weighing an
astonishing 358 lb. It emerged that they had hidden boxes of ammo on
the bus at Changi, and stowed the rounds in their pockets and kit. The
aircraft had taken off 6,000 lb over the maximum weight and still made it,
a testimony to its ruggedness. And the Marines' keenness to maximise
their firepower in the face of the enemy, was taken into account at the
subsequent Board of Enquiry.

On this Labuan Detachment, the 215 Squadron crews rotated every
two weeks. The Airport Hotel had now been wholly requisitioned as the
Officers' Mess, but 215 Squadron's officers were shunted off to the
Membedai Club, now an annexe. Even this was bursting at the seams, and
young Flying Officers had to make do with a camp bed in a corridor, with
nowhere to stow their kit. But at least there was a fan.

The routine was up at 0600, breakfast, Ops for briefing, airborne at
0830, back for a quick lunch before going off on the afternoon sortie, then
an hour's kip before dinner and a few beers. This cycle of sleeping a little,
eating occasionally, and flying a lot was demanding, especially given the
concentration needed over the mountains and DZs. But the landscape was
becoming more familiar and the taller of Batu Lawi's twin peaks, known
as 'The Witch's Tit' to the crews, was a particularly useful landmark.

On a typical morning, the delivery might be eight 1-ton containers at
Rumah Lusong, a small garrison on a riverbank close to the Indonesian
border. It was a straightforward drop, except that the DZ measured just

20 by 30 yards. On average, seven out of eight would land on the target, but if in the one that floated away down-river were 160 gallons of chopper fuel – as happened three times in one drop at Sepulot – there'd be hell to pay from the Army. The afternoon run might be another eight 1-ton containers to Long Pasia, an airstrip with a 300-yard-long grass runway, but in a narrow valley and at that time of day, as often as not, full of cloud and rain. After a couple of attempts at getting in, the Argosy would hang around until it cleared a bit, then set up a tight circuit with no more than half-a-mile downwind and a steep 180-degree turn round onto drop heading. There would then be not much more than a minute to lob the 1-ton container out before climbing furiously away at full power, to avoid the cloud and the hills – and then doing it seven times more.

After days like that, we found, in the time-honoured way, blessed relief from the tension in the bar. One evening, in walked a tall, gaunt figure in tattered jungle greens, looking as though he had spent a week trekking out of the *ulu* – and visibly upset.

In impeccable Sandhurst tones he enquired: 'Is the captain of the Argosy here?'

He was. Steve was built like a lock-forward and not easily intimidated. 'Yeah, what d'you want?'

'Were you dropping at Pa Main last Wednesday?'

Steve nodded. 'Yeah, what about it?'

'You knocked my shithouse down!'

Taken aback, but not for long, Steve asks, 'Were you in it?'

'Well, no.'

'Come and have a beer, then.' And he did.

The same crew, while dropping eight 1-ton containers at Bario, put one through the cookhouse roof. The soldiery was not happy – even less so after Steve complained over the radio: 'There's no pleasing some people!'

It was, after all, a container of cabbages and potatoes.

Some of the stores dropped were extraordinary by anyone's standards. The Gurkha unit at Long Semado reported a plague of rats. For HQ, the obvious solution was to send them some cats. It had been done before when, long before Confrontation a Beverley had dropped twenty of them to the longhouse at Bario, together with four cases of stout for a con-valescing chieftain. So before long, three aloof felines were serenely descending in a harness-pack. They took up residence and the rats retreated for a while, but were soon back in force. What had happened to the cats? No one knew, but the Chinese cook newly arrived at Long Semado seemed to have had some new ideas for the menu.

All the transport crews were accustomed to dropping livestock to the Gurkhas – normally chickens – to satisfy their requirement for freshly killed meat. But they had an annual festival when the head of a bullock would be cut off with one ritual blow. The carcass then provided the feast. It was decided that dropping bullocks from the skies was sadly out of the question but, as second best, three live goats were once parachuted in, to the great joy of the recipients. When, for another Gurkha feast, a Twin Pioneer carried a bullock to the base at Sibu, the Head Man showed his gratitude and high regard for the crew by presenting the Squadron Commander with an Indonesian ear.

Mules, a means of transport for the soldiers on the mountain trails, were regularly dropped by the Beverleys. Occasionally an Argosy was teamed with this mighty aircraft, to drop the blades for bulldozers being delivered by the Bev. It was a sight to see it up in the mountains, flying right up close to a cliff-face, using its huge fin and rudders to turn at the last possible moment, before dropping, like Dumbo, down to the DZ. These were the same crews and aircraft that flew for hours up to Nepal, to land on the mountain airstrip at Kathmandu, collecting newly trained Gurkha reinforcements. In June they very nearly lost an aircraft when, one and-a-half hours out of Calcutta, they ran into the most tremendous storm, with hailstones the size of walnuts. Spiralling down from 9,500 feet, with both pilots struggling with the controls, the Bev pulled out just above the sea, and flying blind all the way, staggered into Rangoon.

Sometimes, for a change from the normal approach into Labuan, a Bev would run in and break. When two of them were serviceable, they'd do this in pairs, thundering in formation over the threshold at not much more than 100 miles-per-hour, and rolling round for a stream landing, stately as galleons.

They got this idea from the fighters, who continued to police the ADIZ. Their vigilance had impressed the Indonesian pilots and not many air incursions were now attempted, so the Javelins and Hunters had to find any potential target they could. One was a missionary in a tiny Cessna, who was startled to have the bulk of a Javelin, missiles, cannon and all, whistling by within feet of his wing tip. Another was an Argosy. Coming back from Tawau, Boss Leary was flying high, at 13,000 feet, to allow Tommy Norcross, the squadron's official photographer, to take some shots of the magnificent towering peaks of Mount Kinabalu – awesome when free of cloud. Coming round the mountain, the Argosy was picked up on radar by Labuan Operations as a possible intruder (the Argosy seldom, if ever, flew that high) and a Javelin was scrambled to intercept. But the Argosy captain had started a max-rate descent to get down to circuit height at Labuan. The Javelin consequently missed its quarry, intercepting clear, blue sky. When the story got out, the Boss was highly gratified at having given the pride of Fighter Command the slip. For a few evenings after, he was king of the bar.

On occasion the crew would get a few hours off, usually when the weather was too bad to fly. Storms could close in on Labuan at speed. Many a time a Borneo mission ended in a mad dash for the runway, or had to be spun out for an hour or so, waiting for the wind and rain to pass. There was no radar assistance at Labuan and in one horrendous storm, when the lightning took out the runway lighting, Dickie Miller and his crew were forced to get the Argosy down, guided by the headlights of two Land Rovers.

Sitting on the verandah at sundown, the crew's first hint of a storm might be a slight movement in the very top of the palm fronds. In no time at all the darkening sky would be plunged into blackness, the heavens would open and down would crash the torrential rain. The sea would be lashed by the wind into foaming waves, sweeping over the coral and up the beach. But the crew wouldn't witness this water show, with its magnificent phosphorescence – they'd be remustering at the first drop of rain in the comfortable safety of the bar.

Recreational possibilities at Labuan were few. There was a station cinema, and swimming – but the bay was not as attractive as it first seemed. In addition to the biting sandflies, a wartime landing craft was slowly rusting away on the beach beside the grave of an unknown Japanese soldier. And right down the middle between the officers' and other ranks' areas ran a sewer pipe. Around the corner was a Sea-Dyak village – picturesque to visit but not served by flush lavatories. So we carried on watching the water from the bar.

An Argosy crew might hire a minibus to see the sights of base. With luck, there'd be a 4- or 5-feet-long monitor lizard to see in the scrub – fierce-looking beasts better faced from inside the vehicle. The town and port of Victoria, where the 'godowns' or warehouses had been taken over as army stores, would not delay them long, but the Hotel Victoria had a passable lounge – a change from the Mess. Out on Surrender Point was a commemoration of the 32nd Japanese Southern Army's surrender to the Australians on 9 September 1945, and close by, the moving memorial to the Commonwealth War Dead, and the Australian Soldiers' Cemetery.

These sombre places brought thoughts of mortality – the transports had had many a close shave but no crashes so far. Supply-dropping was hazardous in the extreme, and every day flown shortened the odds on fatalities. But the fickle fates appeared to favour us, as they did the Comets of RAF Transport Command. One of the Air Movements drivers put his fork-lift truck through the fuselage of a VIP Comet and they threw the book at him. But the official mood changed when it was realised that the incident had served to show how thin the aircraft's skin had become from constant polishing. The discovery probably saved many lives.

Other squadrons were not so fortunate. 'Kiwi' Thompson, who had won the Sword of Honour in our time at Cranwell, tragically flew his Canberra into the sea, over the China Rock firing-range east of Changi, quite possibly losing focus on the glassy surface of the water. The same thing happened to two Javelins one clear, still night. One disappeared, and so did the aircraft that was sent out to investigate.

In another incident, a Scimitar naval fighter diverted from HMS *Ark Royal* to Changi, after one of its two engines failed. Late on final approach, an auxiliary gearbox on the remaining engine failed, leaving neither electrics nor hydraulics, and the aircraft simply fell out of the sky. It bounced once in the undershoot, yawed through 90 degrees as it jumped over the road, and finished upside-down, on fire, next to the Meteor dispersal – narrowly missing nine target-towing aircraft parked on it. Meanwhile, the pilot ejected (horizontally), was fired straight down the runway on his back (still in the seat) – and stood up and walked away. After a quick check over in the Station Medical Centre, he was on his way back to HMS *Ark Royal* in a Gannet.

One month at Labuan was a bad one for flight safety, with three incidents of increasing severity. A Whirlwind helicopter crashed in a mangrove swamp over on the Borneo coast and badly damaged its tail rotor. Labuan fitters made the repairs and the chopper was recovered, despite heavy rain and encroaching tides. A landing Javelin hit the lip of a concrete extension to the runway, burst a tyre and tore off the under-carriage and a Firestreak missile. There was no fire and no casualties, but the aircraft was severely damaged. On another occasion, two Hunters took off in formation on routine patrol, but the leader's aircraft caught fire after take-off. The pilot turned back towards the airfield for an emergency landing. He jettisoned the under-wing tanks but one hung up. At 500 feet there was complete hydraulic failure and the pilot ejected. He was picked up out of the sea by a Whirlwind helicopter, but died four hours later.

By early December 1964, hung-up 1-ton containers had broken so many Argosy rear doors that the squadron had to be withdrawn from the Labuan detachment for a month of running repairs.

The first month of the new year was an eventful one on the political front. Malaysia was elected to the Security Council, whereupon Indonesia stalked out of the UN and upped the tempo in Borneo. The promised Australian and New Zealand troops arrived – the Royal Australian Regiment, and two companies of Australian and New Zealand Rangers (their SAS) and they were soon in action. Japan, Pakistan and Thailand offered mediation and proposed peace talks in Tokyo in May. The Malaysian Tunku said yes – President Sukarno angrily said no.

The same month, news came of Churchill's death. Despite the fact that more armed Indonesians had landed in Singapore, a number of us went downtown to see the newsreels of the funeral. The moving scenes of the barge bearing the great man's coffin up the Thames, and of the cortege to the Abbey, were given added poignancy by being viewed out on the crumbling edge of the old warrior's beloved Empire.

In February, with their doors patched up, the Argosies got back to work out of Labuan. On 27 February, one of the Queen's Flight aircraft brought Prince Philip out on a visit to the Borneo bases. An Argosy was tasked with flying his personal pilot around the DZs in advance, pointing out features of interest, hazards and escape routes before HRH Prince Philip made a four-day tour in his own aircraft. The FEAF jungle rescue team stood by and unfamiliar burly figures appeared, making sure that all went smoothly – but not even they could argue with Sod's Law. The Duke was staying with the Governor in Kuching, at the Astana Palace, but his baggage was sent to the Aurora, a town centre hotel.

At Labuan he was interested in how the Argosy performed. It was explained by the captain, Horse, that it was a great aircraft from a pilot's point of view, but, regrettably, rather underpowered. There could be a bit of bother if an engine failed at the wrong time at the wrong DZ. Prince Philip's response was short.

'I wish the buggers who design these aircraft were made to fly them operationally.'

The Queen's Flight aircrew reported a similar pithy reaction when he noticed some yellow packing cases at Changi which had been hastily and ineffectually camouflaged to keep them from the royal view.

'What the bloody hell have they done that for?'

Very popular, was HRH with the boys in Borneo.

The Army made sure that the Duke was introduced to those largely unsung heroes – now remustered into the Royal Corps of Transport – who packed all the supplies into containers, mounted them onto pallets, attached parachutes, and loaded the whole lot into the aeroplane. In many cases they came along as well and shoved it out. They worked in primitive conditions in stultifying heat and humidity, with unfailing cheerfulness, and earned the affectionate nickname, 'Grunts'.

Reports came in that the Indonesians, notably unimpressed by the royal presence, were mounting major incursions at Bario and Pensiangan. As a precaution the Oerlikon guns at Labuan were brought to permanent alert, and the transport crews had to cut short their hob-nobbing with the Prince to make emergency ammunition drops to the beleaguered troops.

The Argosies of 215 Squadron continued the Labuan Detachment until the middle of August, delivering an average of eighty 1-ton containers a week, with 90 per cent accuracy. In April, the Argosies and Beverleys, in 190 flying hours, dropped 1,355,000 lb of supplies – a record – including a double MSP from an Argosy at Long Akah strip, delivered to within 25 yards of the ident letter. Not much encouragement was needed to keep the crews raising the bar but competition between Beverleys, Argosies and Hastings certainly helped. The Bev could carry 45,000 lb of freight, twice as much as the Argosy, if it used double tiers: one line of 1-tons, carrying another line on an arrangement of rails.

For ten days in September the Argosies returned, the 34 Squadron crews having to go off to Singapore to receive a new Standard, and 215 Squadron, not for the only time, operated out of Kuching and Labuan at the same time. Consumption of spares in the harsh climate was well above the planned level, and shortages had reduced serviceable aircraft to only five of the ten on strength. Training was cut to the bone and two aircraft were borrowed from 105 Squadron in Aden.

Another plaudit was earned from the Labuan Station Commander: 'The fact that these aircraft rarely fail to find their DZ in often fearful weather conditions speaks highly of the crews and their ability and determination to keep the jungle strips resupplied. On many occasions drops are completed in pouring rain, under a low cloud-base and in very bumpy air. Added to this must be the dangers of the mountainous terrain, largely unmapped, in which these operations take place.'

The aircrews couldn't have said it better themselves.

CHAPTER ELEVEN

Sarawak Saga

Twenty months of active service are having their effect on the young aircrew of 215 Squadron. Duffy certainly aged a few years in his slit trench at Tawau, as did a couple of co-pilots who followed in similar month-long postings as Ops Officers: Alan Baker at Long Semado, and Ted Deacon at Labuan. In February 1965, Mike Cross, another of the co-pilots from the Cranwell trio, is sent on a Captains' Course – not bad just two years after we left training at Oakington – and Tom Sneddon becomes the second-highest category navigator on the squadron.

I have the feeling that I'm treading water. I've been carpeted by John Hare, the new Flight Commander in charge of aircrew training, for not reaching the standards expected of a Cranwell graduate. He says I'm less than averagely diligent where my career development is concerned and that I spend too much time in the bar and in the crew-room playing cards. He's right, but my defence is that I've been flying almost continuously and the card games relax the tension. Then in March, as a complete change, and possibly a cunning move by the powers that be, I'm detailed to cover the first three weeks of the Squadron Adjutant's long leave. In any event I'm available as, all at the same time, a leg wound inflicted on the rugby field goes septic, I get double conjunctivitis, and develop mild malaria. At Sick Quarters the doctor has a muscular Malay nurse inject penicillin into my backside with a hypodermic big enough to treat a horse – and I'm grounded.

It's actually very instructive being Adjutant and it gets me out of the crew-room. I've had various supplementary duties over the past year and a half: captain of squadron cricket and Officers' Mess darts, and Entertainments Member at the Mess. This has meant organising the Sunday evening buffet-dances – acquiring the latest Beatles tape and helping to choose the curry. I have spent many a happy afternoon with the girls down at the NAAFI headquarters in Singapore going through their film library and making the week's selection. But this is my first experience of proper Air Force administration and the procedures laid down in detail in

Queen's Regulations. Warrant Officer Shepherd has run the Squadron admin with a rod of iron, ably assisted by the Squadron Clerk, Jack Ord. Jack introduces me to the typewriter – a clunking manual Imperial that produces squadron reports and Daily Orders not entirely free of smudges and corrections, but just about legible. I become party to all sorts of interesting gossip and information. I'm surprised to find there's an armourer on the establishment on account of those bombs and their racks – never required in the event, so the armourer finds other work to fill his time. I get to drive the Adjutant's Land Rover, and knowing exactly where I'm going to be for nearly a month gives me some control over my free time.

On the darts team I meet a couple of pilots off the Target Towing Flight and get the chance of a ride in one of their Meteors. These twin-jet fighters had entered RAF service in the Second World War, and were speedy enough to overhaul V1 flying-bombs and bring them down. They valiantly fought the MiGs in the Korean War but their patchy safety record earned them the gruesome nickname, 'Meatbox'. Swooping and soaring effort-lessly above the Straits makes an exhilarating change from the ponderous Argosy, and I get a whole new view of Changi.

There's also the opportunity to get down to the Padang in Singapore to watch a touring cricket team from Worcestershire play a Malaysian XI – Tom Graveney scores 161.

The next day Tom Sneddon takes over at the Adjutant's desk, and I'm signed off sick parade to report back, refocused, for flying duties. But all the flying I get is a one-way trip to Sibu, in central Sarawak. It's my turn to be an Air Operations Officer.

HQ Midwest Brigade
Sibu
Sarawak

15th April 1965

Dear Charlie,
How are you going? I bet you're surprised to get a letter from me. Well, it's such an extraordinary set-up here that I just had to tell someone about it. And who better than you? You'll know from National Service what kind of surprise can lurk up the military sleeve.

Since I was home last year I've been dicing with death over the jungles of Borneo, defending the Commonwealth and all that. Except for the last three weeks, when I've been down in the jungle living the life of a soldier really – and you'll know all about that too.

I've been snatched away from the comforts of RAF Changi and sent out for a stint as Air Ops Officer at the HQ of the Brigadier who runs the show in this part of Borneo. There's all sorts of soldiery here – two lots of Gurkhas, the Gloucesters, New Zealanders and Malays. We've an armoured squadron of the King's Own Scottish Borderers and a field battery of the Artillery. They say the SAS and the Paras are up-country, and there's a company or two of very brave native Dyaks, called the Sarawak Path Finder Force – local scouts helping to find the bad guys.

I work up at the airfield in the Forward Air Transport Operations Centre – shortens nicely to FATOC. My job's to make sure that the Brigadier's orders feed through to air-supply ops, and to keep him briefed on results. Every evening I've to code up a signal to send down to RAF Ops in Kuching, saying what missions have been flown in the day. We've got a squadron of Whirlwind choppers off the commando carrier HMS *Albion*, and they take troops and supplies up into the jungle where the fighting's going on.

When I flew in, the chap I was relieving (another co-pilot off the squadron) flew out in my place. He'd been here a month – I suppose I will be too. Our landing was pretty hairy – the runway's short (well under a mile) and horribly slippery when it's wet. We had to let the tyres down too, to reduce the wheel loading.

Sibu's on the coastal plain of Borneo – a small market town where two rivers meet. One of them, the Rajang, is the biggest in Sarawak. The whole place is full of water, it rains every day and it's hot and humid as hell. When I arrived I was billeted in a hotel (a pretty basic affair, no air-con) right on the town square, and bloody noisy at night I can tell you, what with the soldiers boozing and chatting up the local talent, and the flaming frogs and insects. The Borneo Club over the square is like something out of Somerset Maugham. They've got a skittle alley and one of the regulars, a big fat English guy (a trader, been here for years) is the ace of the base. When the river floods, the timber floor of the alley warps, and he knows just how it changes shape. Thumping great balls they are too – you should see him hurling them down the alley and falling full-length after them. Wish I had a camera.

Anyway, after a couple of nights, I come down to my Land Rover (it goes with the job) climb in and set off for the airfield. A mile down the road I'm overtaken by the rear off-side wheel! It goes about 50 yards and veers off to the left, straight as a die into the front door of a local's house. I manage to stop, and follow the wheel. Long story short – I fetch the wheel back, meet the daughter of the family (these native girls are fabulous . . .) and get moved out of the hotel and into the Army Officers' Mess. The security guys reckon the wheel's been sabotaged by Indo insurgents – I reckon it's just a wheel nut-case (ho-ho).

These army types certainly know how to live in style. We live in huts but the food and batting are top notch. The other evening we were all taken into town for a slap-up banquet on the Chinese mogul who supplies the Brigade HQ with its victuals. Total bribery and corruption – and thoroughly enjoyable.

There are plenty of creepy-crawlies here. I'm pretty much immune to snakes by now but I cringe at one of the flying beasties called the Borneo beetle. It's like a dragonfly but four times as big. They bombard us after dark in the main Mess building where they get themselves chopped up by the rotating ceiling fans – blood and guts everywhere. There's wire netting over the windows of the sleeping quarters and that keeps most of them out but the noise of their legs and wings is grisly and when you go out to the khasi (no indoor plumbing here, mate) then they've got you.

It's great to meet all these army and navy blokes and get the low down from them on the fighting. Actually, the Navy's very down at the moment and I can't say I blame them. On an operation the other day they lost two of their choppers up river. Came too close into a tight clearing and collided. Eight dead. There's a lot of that out here, Charlie, but we all put it to the back of our minds. Have to. Can't happen to me, and all that.

There's another RAF pilot here, great guy (a Scotsman, but no one's perfect). Jock flies this fantastic machine called a Single Pioneer (made in Scotland too). It's single-engined, with a terrifically long high wing, and it can take off and land on a postage stamp. One of them lost power last month but managed to land on the same road where I lost my wheel. Anyway, I hitched a ride with him yesterday – to Kapit, a smaller town about 50 miles up the river. What an experience! I reckon we didn't once get above the trees on the banks – a low-flying bird's eye view of the jungle. And we landed on what must have been their volleyball court – real flying.

We visited the head man (wearing his best flowery loincloth and rings in his ears) sitting in state in his round-house. We delivered peace offerings (best single malt) from the Brigadier and brought some replacement radio kit and letters to the signals outstation. When we got back to the plane there were dug-out canoes coming down the river to market, carrying a bevy of the local lovelies – in sarongs, with nothing above the waist. Believe it or not, they stood on the riverbank, fished about in their baskets for the bras the missionaries had dished out – and put them on before going into town. Beautiful.

Talking of beauty, I'm off now to visit that pretty Dyak girl who gave me my wheel back. I've no idea when they're coming to get me out of here – just now I hope they don't!

All the very best, and keep a straight bat.

Rog

In the event, an Argosy flew in to get me the very next week, and I reluctantly handed over to a new innocent. At Changi, the squadron was buzzing. The Argosies were having difficulty with serviceability through lack of spares and to meet its flying task, the crews of 215 Squadron were having to operate all hours of the day and some of the night. The Borneo action continued without let-up. At Bau, the 3rd Royal Australian Regiment found itself under attack from the largest incursion in a year, and at Balai Ringin it was the turn of the 2nd Paras to feel the force of *Confrontasi*. Fortunately there was a seasonal break in the monsoon, and the Valettas and Hastings from Kuching dropped two months' average load in just four weeks, right up country, easing the load on the heli-copters.

Reports came from deep in the jungle that an Australian SAS patrol of four men had been charged by an elephant, leaving one badly gored. While one stayed with the injured man the other two managed to reach a forward strip, and a force of thirty Gurkhas was air-lifted into the area. They searched for some days but sadly the casualty died just hours before they found him.

At the end of May, the fighting came uncomfortably close to home. Tanjong Pingelik, 5 miles east of Changi, was the site of Second World War gun emplacements. A courageous (perhaps foolhardy) Indo Army Captain, of the elite *Para Kommando* unit, with just two dozen soldiers, chose these crumbling fortifications as a base from which to mount an assault on Malaya. Unfortunately for them, they were spotted coming ashore by local Malays, and the next day the insurgents and their hill-top were blasted by the cannon of 20 Squadron Hunters. It was quite a show for the spectators at Changi Officers' Club – but catastrophic for the Indonesians. They fought bravely but, their invasion doomed, were mopped up in twelve days.

In June, 215 Squadron was sent out to Kuching again, to support the Valettas and Hastings. The Argosies found they could get 1-ton con-tainers into all but two or three of the Sarawak DZs, and this meant a sizeable increase in the tonnage dropped. But the shortage of new 'chutes led to more 'hard extractions' and cracking of the hydraulic jack securing point on the clam-shell doors. This was fixed by running repairs, but serviceability was a worry. Even so, the Argosy at Kuching flew ninety hours in that first month of the detachment.

At Changi, an Argosy is detailed for a rare operation – a paratroop dropping exercise. There has been no call for airborne assault in this campaign. Dropping on a parachute into very tall trees had been tried in the Malayan Emergency, but discontinued after many broken legs, and several fatalities. Even if the hapless troops made it through the forest canopy in one piece, they were faced with the choice of dangling defence-less from the branches, or attempting the hair-raising climb of a couple of hundred feet down to the jungle floor. There were experiments with abseiling – but the main problem was the inability to carry much kit at all below a parachute. Nevertheless, it is considered important to keep the troops in practice, so exercise 'Windy Weather' is set up, with forty-four lucky lads from the Gurkha Infantry Parachute Company making the drop, at Kuantan.

The aircraft is in para-dropping rig: four rows of sling seats, two against the freight-compartment walls and two back-to-back down the centre. On the first run two 'drifters' go out from the side doors, to assess the wind. They fearlessly make no attempt to steer themselves but nevertheless land just 15 yards from the aiming-point. The first stick of fourteen then follows – seven from each side. At 'Action stations', the Gurkhas hook their static lines to a cable along the wall, and weighed down with 'chute and kit, shuffle forward into line. At 'Red light on', the lead man stands square in the doorway. At 'Green on', he leaps into the void, the rest of the stick following close behind, in an inexorable stamping rhythm that sweeps them all forward and out.

There are seven static lines now streaming back out of the side doors, whipping around in the slipstream. The dispatchers grab them all together and haul them hand-over-hand back into the cabin. After two more runs, and then one for the two dispatchers to get in on the act, the drop's complete.

The aircraft lands and waits while the parachutes are repacked, and then they do it all again. Inevitably, with a fairly strong wind and out-of-practice troops, there are casualties: a broken leg, a fractured wrist, two dislocated shoulders, a broken nose and several sprained ankles. The worst injuries are collected after three Gurkhas collide at 50 feet and drop like stones to the ground. None of them is in the least daunted by all this – even taking in their stride having to repack their own parachutes.

Our great respect for the paras is increased ten-fold for those of us who volunteer to face some of the terrors ourselves in the 'Changi Splash' – a single descent into the sea. The training's bad enough: two days of simulated jumps at the hands of the phyzzies again. The first exercise involves climbing an open ladder 60 feet up a hangar wall, edging along a dizzying platform, and jumping off it fixed by a lanyard to an arrangement of fans, that spin and slow the descent. We repeat this until we get it right. Those who survive – eighteen out of the twenty-four starters – graduate to the next stage. We climb to another 60-feet-high platform and jump from the 'exit trainer'. Fixed to a pulley running on a sloping wire, out we go and make a free descent to the ground some 40 yards away. That simulates a drifting landing, and very realistic it is too. Some ankles don't survive to the next stage, the actual drop the next morning.

At dawn, dolled up in parachute and crash helmet, a dozen of us sit in the barn-like belly of a Beverley, circling over the Straits of Johore, with bowels turning to water and waiting for the moment of truth. The dispatchers have spent the short time since take-off geeing us up for the leap into the void. My name begins with 'A' so I'm in the first stick of two, jumping, as chance would have it, with the Station Padre. The dispatcher calls us to readiness and somehow I force my trembling legs to get me upright, and weighed down by the main and reserve 'chutes, shuffle to the side of the aircraft. With a shaking hand I manage to hook my static line to the cable, while the instructor makes a final check of my equipment. I'm acutely aware that I'm about to trust my life, from 1,200 feet, to this bag of silk on my chest.

The red light of doom comes on, and with the padre behind me, I stumble forward towards the door. With ghoulish glee the dispatcher points down to an island passing below.

'Chinese cemetery,' he yells above the engines' stupendous racket. I manage a sickly grin.

'Face the door!' I stand four-square in the Beverley's side door, with the padre praying audibly behind me.

'Green on!' and with the dispatcher's broad hand pushing at my back, I commit myself to fate and plunge out into the slipstream.

There's a sudden silence as the Beverley sails away, and a moment of floating weightlessness as the body rides the warm morning air. It can't be more than a second or two, but it's never forgotten. Then there's a jolt as the static line tugs out the 'chute and I'm heavy again, but mercifully hanging from the blessed brown dome of silk up there above my head. I'm saved. I've done it. Look at me flying!

The view is marvellous – the dawn sky, the sun-dappled sea, and the other 'chute up there above me. The padre's now launched into a triumphant hymn.

He who would valiant be, 'gainst all disaster
Let him in constancy, follow the Master!

I'm so enthralled that I completely forget to release the reserve 'chute on its lanyard to give a marker for height above the water, and to prepare the main 'chute quick-release for when I plummet into the sea. So in I go, 'chute and all, and find myself thrashing about under acres of sodden silk, struggling to get free. Fortunately, there's a launch standing by for just such an occurrence and within moments I'm being hauled over the side.

'Come along, Sir. Let's have you. Forget your quick-release box, did you, Sir? There's always one ...'

Undignified but exhilarated, I wait for the padre, beaming from ear to ear, to join me, and we watch the rest of the drops, relaxed and self-satisfied. We've been initiated into a rare and unforgettable experience.

In the second week of July, there comes the sad news that a Hastings has crashed near Abingdon, with the loss of all the crew. The inquiry finds that metal fatigue has caused a bolt in the tail to shear, jamming the elevators. As a result, all Hastings aircraft, worldwide, are grounded. This means a sharp increase in work for the Argosies.

At the same time, two years after the squadron reformed at Changi, re-cycling of the crews starts. The arrival of new, inexperienced men, and the need to run air-supply detachments – currently from both Labuan and Kuching– gives even more for us old Borneo hands to do.

I find myself back at Kuching the day after the Hastings crash. As it's all hands to the pumps, the crewing system has been shelved and I'm on a scratch team. Andy Adams is the captain, now experienced in the hazards of tactical transport ops. In December last year his Argosy's nose wheel failed to come down on the approach to Kuching. On landing, its casing was torn away, allowing the now exposed wheel to roll quite nicely along the runway. The groundcrew jacked the aeroplane up where it was and locked the undercarriage down. Andy then flew the damaged machine at reduced speed back to Changi for repairs.

Horse is here too, having got the job, together with Dickie Miller, of checking the pilots into the new Sarawak DZs. Tony Ewer, the navigator, is another married man, and as the only bachelor I'm a bit concerned that the social side of life might prove a touch thin. But we move into the Officers' Mess and find on the other side of a volleyball court, a brand-new and identical Sergeants' Mess. On Horse's initiative, permission is given for the two Messes to socialise and on our first evening the Officers visit the Sergeants for cribbage and an arcane version of whist known as 'kirkey'. This has something to do with avoiding the Queen of Spades, but it all gets hazy as the Tiger beer flows. Whilst the engineer, Ken 'Parky' Parkinson, shuffles the deck with a practised flourish, we get into a deep and meaningful discussion with the AQM, Geoff Longmuir, as to what crates of Gurkhas' chickens might weigh if all the birds inside them got airborne at the same time ....

Most evenings are like that. The Sergeants visit us the next night, and so it goes for the fortnight. By day, it's the usual summer monsoon routine of fitting two or three, and sometimes four, missions around the morning low cloud and afternoon storms.

Hostilities are still raging and on one side of the runway threshold stands one of our batteries of MK 1 Bloodhound air defence missiles. They're radar-controlled and for practise, track our aircraft as they take off and land. It's good to see them working, but unnerving all the same.

Because of the risks we run in the air, we're instructed to wear canvas jungle boots, 'chutes and side-arms. We reckon that the chances for both aircraft and crew of surviving a Borneo crash are infinitesimal, and that baling out would leave us suspended in the tree canopy with our boots 300 feet off the ground. So, after negotiations with the Flight Safety officer, the whole lot's consigned to a sturdy box bolted to the Argosy floor. Honour is satisfied all round.

A bombshell is dropped on 9 August when Singapore announces it's leaving the Malaysian Federation. It seems that the tension between the largely Chinese Singapore and the Malay-centric Malaya has finally forced the two apart. There are more riots in Singapore and the slow golfer, Lee Kwan Yew, is installed at Changi again. President Sukarno steps up his propaganda, citing the weakness of Malaysian ties, but is trumped by Singapore's confirmation that she will still commit troops to the struggle and allow continuing use of the Sovereign Base by the British. It's a sensitive time.

With the Hastings still grounded and the shortage of co-pilots, in August I find myself in Kuching again with yet another assorted crew. Off Transport Command Britannias (the 'white-gloves' school of flying) the captain is 'Tommy' Thompson, a stickler for the book – and an aficionado of sautéed kidneys and cheroots at pre-dawn breakfasts. Duffy brings his no-nonsense attitude to the navigator's job, and at the occasional moment of friction Warrant Officer Howarth's authority and experience calm things down. The detachment is different too, for the Valettas of the RAF give way to the Bristol Freighters of 41 Squadron Royal New Zealand Air Force, and their aircrews bring a distinctive brand of mayhem to the Mess – and of bravery in the air.

The Bristol Freighter – known to all as the Bristol Frightener – has two large Hercules radial piston engines on a high, strut-braced wing. At all stages of flight it's pushed to go at much more than 100 miles-per-hour, and it doesn't climb very high. It carries harness packs, which the dispatchers manhandle out of the side doors. The Kiwis are an extra-ordinarily friendly bunch and they invite us along to experience the ride of a lifetime in their machine, warning us that the wings of one of their aircraft actually once collapsed in the wind-shears of Christchurch.

It's appallingly noisy. Mounted inside the door is a small box with cotton-wool earplugs for general use as the fuselage, an aluminium tin-can, shudders and booms to the vibration of the props. *En route*, the navigator perches on a shelf at the back of the flight deck and transfers to the nose for the drop. When it rains, water pours down the instrument panel. They drop at the DZs near the border, well within range of those threatening anti-aircraft guns – sitting ducks. On an earlier mission an incendiary went through the 'O' ident letter on the nose, took out a radio, damaged the toilet and started a fire in a parachute. The guys on the ground, Commandos, Gurkhas and Marines, love them for battling through in all weathers.

We, together with the Javelin, Hunter and naval helicopter aircrews, love them too for bringing a breath of fresh air into the Mess. They're great songsters, their lyrics having a particular Antipodean charm.

Flying down to Sarawak, in a Kiwi 'plane,
Flying down to Sarawak, in the pouring rain.
Flying down to Sarawak, my guts are in a whirl
Flying down to Sarawak, my God I'm going to hurl!

The Station Commander at Kuching is an Australian Wing Commander, known to friend and foe alike as 'Blue' – and among his foes he can certainly count the Kiwis. He's really quite a decent bloke, with the Distinguished Flying Cross to boot – but he has recklessly installed an ornamental fishpond between the officers' accommodation blocks. It's a perfect breeding ground for mosquitoes and to the Kiwis, a magnet for mischief. They mount a campaign on this pond, usually relieving themselves in it on the way back after an evening of chilli crabs and Tiger beer in Kuching Market. That is, if they haven't fallen into the monsoon drain before they get there. The *coup de grâce* for the fish comes in the form of a cataclysmic Dambusters raid, complete with music and a thunderflash.

But no one begrudges them their exuberant relaxation – they earn it in the air. Boss Leary's crew were returning from a successful drop when they picked up, on the emergency frequency, a Mayday call from the NZ crew. They'd lost an engine during a drop. The Argosy could see them, deep in an ascending valley and chucking everything except the pilot out of the doors, trying desperately to gain some precious height. They just managed to turn and, guided by the Argosy – also acting as a radio relay – found a path through the hills and staggered back to base. 'Frightener' indeed.

I seem to have gained a reputation as a reasonably useful pilot-navigator. Names on the chart are instantly recognisable: *bukit* is a hill, *batu* a rock, *gunong* a mountain and *sungei* a river. I've developed a mental map of Sarawak and can find my way following rivers, mountains, hills, caves, villages and pepper plantations – just as long as we keep under and out of cloud. I hope I've squared my account with the Flight Commander Flying, and shown myself in a better light.

Just after the Battle of Britain parade in September, when the squadron flags are carried in review past the Spitfire mascot at Changi, and it rains so hard the accompanying fête is abandoned, I'm asked to 'volunteer' for another detachment. I find myself at Kuching for the third time in as many months, with Horse as captain and Art as navigator. Both are now among the most experienced supply-dropping operators on the squadron and in the air, we certainly maintain the standards for tonnage dropped, and for accuracy. We probably set new standards for high spirits on the ground – Parky's on the crew, and the Kiwis beat all records for wild behaviour.

Mike Keane, one of their navigators, tells a story in the bar. No. 41 Squadron had been at Changi since the Malayan Emergency, when the New Zealand Army fought alongside the Brits. One of their Dakotas went up the wrong valley and hit a ridge with the loss, so the search team thought, of the whole crew. But the Sergeant dispatcher had survived and was taken in by the natives. By the time he managed to drag himself away from their tender loving care and find his way out of the jungle, the squadron had already given him a military funeral. Today's Kiwis are an equally oddball assortment. More than one is usually in trouble, charged with *grand prix* driving, riot or insubordination. Life's a lot livelier when they're around.

A shot of the Kiwi spirit is just what's needed as nerves on the base are getting somewhat frayed. It's a dangerous time for low-level flying as the seasonal jungle burning in Indonesia has reduced visibility to less than 1,000 yards. A Scout helicopter of the Army Air Corps with a crew of three has disappeared in the jungle and can't be found, even after two weeks of looking. One of the search Whirlwinds has disappeared too. We watch a Whirlwind with buckled rotors being carried into Kuching, slung under the belly of a Belvedere. The Javelins develop cracks in their tail-planes and are replaced by Australian Sabres. But the Kiwis keep on singing, the Hastings fleet gets airborne again, and we manage a smile or two when, on a mission up at Long Jawi, the DZ controller comes on the air.

'Four-four-six, that one was a bit off line. You know that longhouse down by the hill? It's now two short-houses.'

The strain of the constant round of flying, drinking, singing and flying again – on a diet of bacon butties, and those aromatic poached eggs – is beginning to tell. We've been at this for months and I'm losing track of time and loosening my hold on reality. Will it ever end?

On the last day of September, a light appears at the end of the tunnel. Out of the blue, or so it seems to us up at the sharp end, there's a Communist-inspired coup in Djakarta. Has President Sukarno been deposed? What do we all do if peace breaks out?

On my return to the squadron a couple of days later, the Adjutant hands me a buff envelope. Inside is a typewritten sheet telling me I'm to be posted, to Central Flying School in England, to become a flying instructor. I'm rather pleased – my flying and 'officer qualities' must have come on a bit to get me selected to train new pilots. But it's difficult to grasp that my momentous adventures in the Far East are to come, after all, to an end.

CHAPTER TWELVE

Farewell

The newspapers in Temple Hill Officers' Mess are full of the mayhem in Djakarta. In the Communist coup, a number of Army Generals are murdered. In retaliation, right-wing leaders of the armed forces mount a counter-coup, and the Army is dominant again, but no one's sure of President Sukarno's fate. The mob runs amok, burning down the Communist headquarters. How strong is the Indonesian will to continue the struggle? Strong enough it seems, for the message coming out of Djakarta is that *Confrontasi* continues. Air incursions intensify. A B-26 crosses the border near Bario, machine-gunning the native villages – certainly not an action designed to win the battle for hearts and minds. South of Kuching, the Gurkhas fight half-a-dozen engagements. In one of them, Lance Corporal Rambahadur Limbu, of the 10th Princess Mary's Own Gurkha Rifles, wins the Victoria Cross.

But the new co-pilots are checked out now, and I'm no longer required on Borneo detachments. With my posting date, 19 December, just a few weeks away, that suits me. I have to try to get mentally tuned to a return to service life in England. Anyway, I've a lot to fit in.

First, there's the panic tan. Postings have been coming through for three months now, and one by one chaps on the list can be seen, towel under arm, trudging down to the Officers' Club to acquire the bronzed look that's expected of a returning warrior. It takes a lot of hard work as the autumn monsoon clouds keep the sun at bay. But the effort has to be made – even by those whose exposure to it to date has been limited to the walk from *basha* to bar.

Then, there are promotion exams to take. To make Flight Lieutenant in the New Year's list, I need to pass papers in Administration and Organisation, Air Force Law, General Service Knowledge, Flying and Airmanship and Air Operations. It's daunting, but a number of us are in the same boat and peer pressure carries us through.

The exams are in the Education Block, one of a line of barrack-style buildings that includes the Airmen's Mess. On refurbishment of this Mess, under the whitewashed walls was found a remarkable series of paintings, which came to be known as the Changi Murals. Depicting religious themes, they were the work of a British prisoner of the Japs, painted twenty years ago. They are now being restored by an artistic type out from London, an unassuming soul, apparently gratified to be staying in the Officers' Mess. He's known to us all as Stanley. It turns out he's Stanley Warren, the painter of the murals. A Royal Artillery Bombardier in the Second World War and now a schoolmaster, he is due a great deal of respect.

After the exams Tom and I are looking for a bit of light relief.

'They say that if I don't take the rest of my leave now, I'll lose it.'

'Right then, Rog, let's take the MG for a proper look up the East Coast.'

On an earlier trip this year, to our favourite getaway, the Kota Tinggi waterfalls, my old Riley gave up the ghost. It had not been happy for some time, and something had been knocking in the engine most of the way back. A couple of miles short of Changi, that something came right through the crankcase – a con-rod, complete with pulverised piston. The car was good for nothing but scrap. I was sad, but consoled by acquiring Tom's 1952, red MG TD sports model. It was hopelessly uneconomical – doing only 18 miles to the gallon, it was cheaper to take a taxi. I fancied the idea of a motorbike – Pat had done very well with his Honda moped, sailing along the Changi roads, dodging the traffic if not the rain. But I bought the MG, which, although equally useless in the wet, did great things, I reckoned, for a bloke's image.

We drive 250 miles to Kuantan, through 100 miles of virgin jungle to start with, swerving to avoid the logging lorries that race two-abreast down the narrow road, loaded with massive tree trunks. The car is a health and safety hazard on wheels – the miniscule luggage space behind the seats is crammed with cans full of petrol. We've agreed to be a refuelling bowser for Ginger Lewis. A slight chap, Ginger's built for the cockpit and is absolutely hooked on flying. When he's not being an Argosy co-pilot, he's down at the Singapore Flying Club at Paya Lebar, airborne in whatever he can lay his hands on. Today it's a two-seat Chipmunk, which he wants to take up to a remote landing-ground south of Mersing. For that he needs to organise a fuel supply, and we are it.

We find the isolated strip, not much more than a clearing in the jungle. Stopping by the gate, miles from anywhere, within minutes we're surrounded by locals trying to sell us sugar cane, watermelon and cold Fanta. Where did they come from? How did they know we were here?

After half an hour there's the familiar clatter of a Gipsy engine, and a Chipmunk appears through a gap in the trees, wings vertical. There's a good deal more of that sort of split-arse stuff before it lands. It's Ginger with an unexpected passenger – Ginny. He's been showing her the off-shore islands – in particular the spectacular Pulau Tioman, believed by many of us to be the location for the Bali Hai shots in *South Pacific* – and apparently all at zero feet. Ginny smiles bravely but looks a bit pale as Ginger, with the bit between his teeth, roars off with her back to civilisation.

After a day or two in Mersing we continue along the coast road with miles of palm-fringed, empty beaches. We spend most of the time away swimming, topping up our tans, climbing for coconuts and drinking the cool, sweet milk. Clambering over the rocks and exploring the jungle, we revert to being schoolboys. It's the perfect antidote to Confrontation.

Back on duty, I have a trip up to Thailand. Is this my end-of-tour bonus – one last chance for a night-stop? We take the usual contingent of Royal Engineers, to the newly operational airfield surreptitiously built for the Americans at Mukhadan, now known as Leong Nok Tha. The US action up there is rapidly becoming more intense and Aussie Mirages have joined the fray alongside the USAF. The captain tells us that the last time he was waiting here, an F-100 Super Sabre came limping in, as full of holes as a colander and spouting fuel and oil through every one of them. The pilot pulled off the runway onto the dirt, climbed out and staggered to safety. Today we can see the Sabre, written off and still there.

On the way back, I make my sixteenth visit to Bangkok's airport, before taking off resignedly for Changi. The inevitable wall of thundercloud is looming up ahead, when miracle of miracles, an oil temperature gauge rises beyond limits. It's the critical number three engine, the one with the hydraulic pump and generator. We feather and turn back for the airfield. This is it. At last – a night-stop in Bangkok. Springing out onto the tarmac I join the engineer in examining what, I dearly hope, will entail hours of extensive repair work. One look is enough. There, lodged in the oil-cooler is – a plastic bag. It's quickly removed, the engines are restarted and we take off again for Changi. So near, and yet so far.

Back at the Mess, of course the bar's closed.

A chance comes to say goodbye to Hong Kong. Since April, the storm-tossed and weather-beaten Argosies have been flown up there, one every month, for some tender loving care from HAEC. My name comes up on the roster just at the right time to get in some cold-weather clothes shopping before going home to the creeping damp of England. The Wing

Pilot, Gerry Garforth, is on the trip, riding on the jump seat ready to route-check the captain.

On the way, we see at first-hand how alarmingly the hostilities are developing in Vietnam. In March, President Johnson sent in the Marines in retaliation for Viet Cong raids on American bases. There are now 125,000 US troops in the country, seeking to enforce their President's July declaration: 'We will not surrender and we will not retreat.' We've read about continuous carrier-based bombing raids, and of bombs in Saigon. One exploded in the Tan Son Nhut airport terminal so we've extra cause to be anxious on the approach.

It's the usual pandemonium getting in, a free-for-all among scores of aircraft in the air and on the ground – C-130 transports, B-52 bombers and hundreds of choppers. Then there's the US controller, delivering his fast and frantic messages with an impenetrable accent. If we don't pick up his instruction first time and act on it right away, then we're lost. We risk having to go round again – through choppers suddenly rising like swarms of angry wasps, scrambled fighters cutting across our nose, and PanAm 707s, Cessnas and Bird-dogs landing or taking off on the cross-runway. We did that once and we don't want to do it again. Today I acknowledge the controller's message – whatever it was – and we plough on through the lot, regardless. At about 1,000 feet we watch in amazement as a C-124 flies across our nose, at the same level dropping paratroops.

Our skipper grabs the transmit button.

'Mike Oscar Golf to Saigon control. This is a damn silly time and place to be doing para training! Over.'

Back comes a Southern drawl.

'That ain't no training, Oscar Golf.'

On the ground the chaos continues and we're glad to reach the sanctuary of the terminal. The liaison officer's changed. The new man tells us that his glass-eating predecessor was posted to Twin Pioneers in Singapore, and soon afterwards messed up a fuel cross-feed switching *en route* for Kuching. Both engines stopped and he finished up in the drink. He also tells us that the number of American military aircraft now at Saigon is greater than the strength of the RAF world-wide.

We clamber back into the air, only to find ourselves in the middle of a hundred helicopters lifting an airborne brigade into action at Da Nang. For an hour, over the Vietnamese mainland, flying over places with names fast becoming known around the world – Dalat, Nha Trang and Qui Nhon on the coast – the scars of battle are plain to see. There's no holding back on the air-strikes here – F101 Voodoos and Crusaders run in below, their flaming napalm bombs scorching the undergrowth. Whatever may be the rights and wrongs of this conflict, low profile it certainly isn't. I think of our SAS and Gurkhas in the jungles of Borneo: silent, restrained – and effective.

We get an unexpected extra day off in Hong Kong, waiting to air-test the aircraft we've come to collect. The weather is giving cause for concern. Last month a Hastings was unserviceable at Kai Tak, with one engine out of commission. But a typhoon was forecast so its intended passengers were left behind and it took off on three engines. It made it, which is more than could be said for a C-130 Hercules transport of the USAF, full of servicemen on R and R from Vietnam. From dispersal, Boss Leary watched as the pilot (possibly after a heavy night on the town) tried to take off with one engine accidently in reverse. The Hercules spiralled into the sea and all on board were killed.

It's not surprising then, that the mood at RAF Kai Tak is somewhat sombre. We decide that this is the time for a day-trip to Macau, 40 miles west along the coast, and reported by our mates as being the Portuguese equivalent of Hong Kong. We travel by hydrofoil, which we agree is like being strapped into a civil airliner running over cobbles. But it gets us there quickly and safely enough.

We have a look around at the Sino-Portuguese waterfront, and the cathedral with its elaborate, sculptured façade. But it's not long before we're playing the tables at one of the casinos, Macau's main attraction. Our money goes like water but we cheer ourselves up with a leisurely three-hour trip back to Hong Kong on the SS *Fat Shan*, a small, comfortable ferry that offers a steamer chair, ice-cold bottles of San Miguel beer, and a seascape like no other. This beats the bruising hydrofoil. It's night as we cruise back into Hong Kong harbour, Kowloon and the Island ablaze with millions of lights. It's cold, but the moon and stars are crystal clear in the sky, and the harbour glitters with ships. This is the way to take my leave of the Colony.

But I can't go without a final night in Kowloon. The whole crew is there, including Gerry Garforth. Well under the influence of Tsingtao beer, he takes me confidentially by the arm.

'You should be a B-cat, Rog. You're not doing yourself justice. Why don't we give it a real go tomorrow? Show me what you can do.'

'Right-ho, Gerry. Anything you say, old chap. Look forward to it.'

We drink to that.

The next day I clamber on board the Argosy dragging a hangover and a new grip full of heavy winter clothes, and ready for a route-check. Gerry's been a star on the Temple Hill darts team so I'm hopeful of sympathetic treatment. It's not offered of course, but I've taken extra care with the radio log and I've a good few hours to demonstrate crisp RT procedures and technique – and my instrument flying.

There's plenty of that right away and my hangover's soon a distant
memory. We take off to the south and are into cloud at 500 feet. We lock
on to a back-beam to the Kai Tak beacon, and the GCA (Ground Controlled Approach) radar controller monitors our progress through the
Gap. The captain hands over to me for the climb and I fly on instruments
until we break through the cloud at 15,000 feet.

We continue the climb to 20,000 feet and cruise back over Vietnam. The
Boss, on his trip last month, had pressurisation failure as the Argosy
climbed through the Gap, and had to stay down at 10,000 feet all the way
– not the most convenient height for crossing a war zone. The US air
traffic controllers were understandably suspicious and sent up the inter-
ceptors. A pair of sinister Sabres, bristling with Sidewinder missiles, swept
past the wing tip. It took some rapid RT exchanges to clear the Argosy
through the air defence screen.

Neither our engines nor our airframe break down, flying into and out of
the Vietnam maelstrom. This means that yet again there's no chance of
seeing downtown Saigon and its fabled typically French, tree-lined
boulevards – to say nothing of its graceful, butterfly-like girls. But at least
I get back to Changi with a green instrument rating. There are three levels
in the RAF – white, green and master green – so I haven't done badly. For
the trip overall, I maintain my 'C-cat', and I'm happy with that.

Tom comes back with a poignant account of a trip he's just made to
Tonga. Everyone remembers the magnificently proportioned Queen Salote
who lit up the Coronation procession of our own Queen. His crew, called
out overnight and augmented by a Squadron Leader doctor, a nursing
sister and medical orderly, were detailed to carry the elderly monarch
from Tonga to Fiji. From there, an RAF Transport Command Britannia
was to take her on to hospital in New Zealand. The Brit couldn't get into
the crushed coral and grass airstrip at Tongatapu, a dot in the Pacific two
and-a-half hours south-east of Fiji. But the Argosy could – once it had
found the runway through the 100-feet palm trees, in the rain.

At Nuku'alofa, the Queen's younger son, Prince Tu'ipelehake, welcomed the crew, and garlanded them with frangipani and orchids. There
was a feast in honour of 'The Argosy Visit to Tonga' – roast suckling
pig, chickens, beef, crab, prawns, yams, taros, sweet potatoes, coconut
milk and a salad of every fruit they'd ever seen and some they hadn't. A
government dignitary gave a speech.

'We welcome you as envoys from Queen Elizabeth ... we will show you
our island, to see and enjoy as your own ...' ending on a painfully
touching note, '... we wish you could be here in more pleasant circum-

stances. However, you are here to take our Queen to New Zealand. We love our Queen very much – please, please take care of her.'

The Tongans were an open, friendly and relaxed people and on the day of the Queen's departure they lined the roads all the way to the airport. They were simply and honestly devoted to her and today they were there to watch her going away, care of Queen Elizabeth. Only her family and government officials knew that she was going to hospital in New Zealand, and would probably never again be seen alive in Tonga.

The Argosy crew lined up to be introduced before marching smartly off to the aircraft, and Queen Salote, now frail, tired and very ill, boarded determinedly on her own two feet. Taxiing out for take-off, Tom says, was perhaps one of the most moving moments of his life: the Queen's standard flying from the aeroplane, a band playing sad farewell music and the crowd waving goodbye to their Queen, not knowing it was for the last time.

When Tom told this story, we understood a good deal more about the spirit of Commonwealth. The commitment of the Aussies and New Zealanders in Borneo stood out in stark contrast with the cynicism we were witnessing in Vietnam.

There remain three tasks for me before my flight home. First, I have to go down to the Government Telecommunications Department to book a radio-telephone call to England. I need to tell my brother I'm coming home. Singapore in 1965 is still pretty remote and a good deal of post gets lost both ways.

Then I have to hand over my radio programme. Changi is blessed with a Broadcasting System (known as CBS, naturally, but not quite as famous) and for some weeks now, on Saturday evenings, I've enjoyed presenting a music and chat show, 'Records at Random'. I've taken it over from two mates on 48 Squadron – one was posted and the other got married. They in turn had taken it over from the previous hosts – a Flying Officer WRAF and a Corporal. Their relationship had developed into something more than the strictly professional, and they were sent back to the UK. Sharpish.

Finally, I need to sell my cherished MG. It's snapped up gleefully by Brawn Nicolle, but before he can take delivery it's borrowed by a would-be Stirling Moss to take part in an impromptu reverse-gear road race around the Officers' Mess perimeter road. Predictably, my motor ends up in the monsoon drain, but the deal is honoured and compensation is paid by the bloke who climbs out of the wreckage.

This escapade is one of many hare-brained events that have become common in the Mess over the past few months. As the Indonesian conflict moves into its fourth year, what might be called combat fatigue sets in and aircrews seek more frequent relief in riotous fun and games in the bar. Fuel is added to the flames by a string of farewell parties for officers posted as crews get recycled.

My party is fixed for my very last day at Changi. British Eagle Britannias are running the trooping flights and mine leaves from Paya Lebar at midnight. After a final blow-out at Mr Lim's with the Cranwell trio, Tom, Duffy and the rest, we bowl into the bar, intent on spending my last dollars in style.

There's nothing to guarantee a party quite like the prospect of a departing bachelor buying a jug or two. Soon the night is filled with the raucous voices of half-a-dozen homesick New Zealanders, leading a score or more of us in the favourite Borneo songs.

O, Lee Kwan Yew
O, Lee Kwan Yew
Sing Merdeka! for the Kiwis
Lee Kwan Yew

The Sound of Music has been a great hit with the lads and a small chorus renders their version of *Edelweiss* – dripping with schmaltz – with the whole crowd led by Horse coming in on cue for the Big Finish. Pat's a star turn. In a reedy baritone he gives us a 'Baleeee Hai' that just here and there might have been as Messrs Rodgers and Hammerstein intended.

The men of 215 Squadron decide it's time for the Co-pilot's Lament.

As a lad I served a year or three as co-pilot on an Argosy
I polished the windows and I swept the floors
And switched the switches on the clam-shell doors.
I switched the switches so carefully
But still I'm a co-pilot on the Argosy ...

Mike Tom, a long-range Hastings pilot off Far East Communications Squadron responds with a heartfelt rendition of his favourite march.

See them fly by
Beverleys, Argosies and Hastings
High in the sky
Who's the one, who's the one we adore?
Hastings it's you ...

He's enveloped in a scrum and loses his trousers.

For culture, there's a chap off the Shacks who does an uncanny Laurence Olivier impression, with a series of Shakespearean monologues.

'Shalt I compare thee to a brewer's dray? Thou art more ugly and less temperate ....'

Chairs get organised for the Dambusters' raid: six of us as the crew, sitting one behind the other (front gunner, bomb aimer, pilot, navigator, signaller, and rear gunner) and four of us side-by-side as the engines (left and right inner and outer). We fly the whole mission. Take-off (throttles open, all four engines waving their arms and roaring) and low-level transit across Holland and the Ruhr (machine-gunners driving off German fighter attacks – 'doopha, doopha, doopha'). Then the bombing-run ('Down, down – steady – this is bloody dangerous. Bomb gone!') and the triumphant mission-accomplished signal ('Nigger – Nigger – it's Nigger!'). Finally, the hazardous return flight (engines failing one by one and falling off their chairs) and the emergency landing (crew sprawling in exhausted exhilaration). The entire show has the backing of the stirring film-score, courtesy of the assembled company. There isn't a dry eye in the place.

Through it all, over in a corner, in a world of his own, Robin Cane of 48 Squadron – the amiable guy who taught me to drive on the dispersals at Oakington – is teetering on a stool. With tears streaming down his cheeks, he performs, in a quavering falsetto, the entire score and script of *The Sound of Music*. Julie Andrews, eat your heart out.

Just in time, my pals remember that I'm supposed to be checking-in at Paya Lebar, half-a-dozen miles away. I also remember that I haven't packed yet. Off we troop down the hill to my *basha*. Dot Priest helps me chuck all my stuff into a couple of bags. My treasured tropical fish-tank I solemnly bequeath to Robin, the maestro.

The whole mob then forms three ranks and marches past while I take an emotional salute, the laughter and mock drill commands of my parading comrades-in-arms rising into the perfumed Changi air. I don't want to leave the squadron, the mates and all the glories of the Far East, and I can't really believe I'm going. But an RAF posting notice has to be obeyed. Barry and Dot pour me into their Sunbeam and drive me off to the airport and the waiting Britannia. I'm *en route* again, for the UK and Central Flying School, facing the prospect of Christmas in the grim greyness of an English winter. But what a way to go. What a party.

CHAPTER THIRTEEN

Return

The Malaysian Airways Boeing 737 swoops over the deltas of the Sarawak coast, between the two headlands and over the floodplains to land at the airport south of Kuching. It's 29 January 1998 and this year Chinese New Year coincides with *Hari Raya*. With my wife, I'm taking the opportunity of a few days off from a business trip to Kuala Lumpur to visit Kuching. I've not been there for over thirty years.

We step out of the cool of the airliner into the mid-afternoon sunshine. The heat hits like a sauna and the smell and humidity are exactly as they were when Argosies and Hastings landed here. Wonder of wonders, there to the south rise those same spiky hills. Of course they do – they've been there for millions of years, but it still seems miraculous, after half a lifetime, to see them.

A taxi takes us out of town to the Santubong resort. Twenty miles north of Kuching, by the sea, it's right under Tanjong Sipang, the jungle-clad mountain headland where we dropped supplies on the beach. Here, there's now a holiday village, with golf course and a major hotel. Our room is in a galleried block, polished wood floors underfoot, ceiling fans overhead, and trees and shrubs right outside the window – not so very different from our *bashas*. The sounds of the night that send us off to sleep are familiar echoes.

After an early dip in the outdoor pool the next morning, we follow the signs round the golf course and along the shore to the 'Cultural Village'. This is a landscaped area of several acres, laid out with the longhouses I used to visit in the Borneo jungles. The many different types are here – from small Kelabit rice-huts to the impressive structures of the Land Dyaks, 100 yards long, with a wide central walkway and wood fires smoking under cooking pots. There are old women crouching on the sleeping mats, blowpipes on the walls, and little children scurrying around our knees. At the end stands a round-house, complete with shrunken heads. This is the real thing.

But of course it isn't. It's a reconstruction, although authentic in its detail and character. Outside one of the houses on stilts, a group of young Ibans performs a native dance. To the beat of a drum and music from a pipe the delightful young girls skip gracefully over and between two heavy lengths of bamboo slapped together at ankle height by strapping youths. It's spellbinding. Afterwards they gather round, wanting to practise their English, which, of course, they are all learning at college in Kuching. This is just their pocket money job. None of them is old enough to know anything about *Confrontasi* and they're bemused by this very tall Englishman's stories of exploits over and in the jungle. But they smile politely as my wife tactfully leads me away.

In the evening we eat in the open air at a simple seafood restaurant along the coast, built out over the sea on a rickety pier. This really is the real thing – satay, hum, chilli crab, tiger prawns, and all the right kinds of noodle and Tiger beer. I'm a hungry young pilot again. Our host (I'm reminded of Mr Lim) is pleased to welcome us – not many Europeans find their way to his establishment. He solemnly leads us into his living room, where a large television screen dominates the space. His daughter experiments with her idiomatic English and offers us oranges and sweets in celebration of Chinese New Year. As we climb into our taxi, thanking him for his hospitality, his kitchen hand roars off on his moped – transport now readily available to the young bloods of Borneo.

For the native boys of the 1960s such mobility would have been a dream. The lowland Ibans, Land and Sea Dyaks, got around on foot and in canoes. The mountain Muruts, blowpipe-hunting nomadic Punans, and the Kelabits up on the magic plateau of Bario went just on foot. Tom Harrisson, DSO, OBE describes these people, their beliefs and culture in his book *World Within*, the story of his mobilisation in 1944 and 1945, of the tribes against the Japanese occupiers. He was later Curator of the Sarawak Museum and on four detachments to Kuching I never managed to visit it. On this trip we do, and find a treasure trove of traditional Borneo life – a hidden world in all its richness and intricacy, invisible from 1,000 feet in an Argosy.

We walk into Kuching town centre to eat at the open-air market, as the crews did so often. Do I remember it being this ramshackle and fetid? At the Sultan's palace over the Sungai Sarawak, it's Open House today, to celebrate the season. The old, slow sampan ride is now motorised and takes only a few minutes, but the river is just as muddy and crowded. Wedged in among the families, my hairy arms and legs are still objects of fascination for the children. In the landscaped gardens that once belonged to the Governor, we mingle in the rain with hundreds of smiling and apparently contented locals – couples, grandparents and children all together. A colourful spread of traditional and imported treats (including the ubiquitous Coca-Cola) is there for everyone to enjoy. It's good to see this democratic gathering.

We don't get to Labuan but I know from my business dealings that it's now the offshore financial centre of Malaysia, and doing very well. Nor do we make it to Sabah, but friends tell us that Mount Kinabalu has a tourist park and a well-trodden trail. The ravages of the loggers, so rampant in Sarawak, are being kept at bay, and there are a dozen nature reserves across the State, where orang-utans, hornbills and gibbons survive.

As we fly out of Kuching for Singapore we think of our daughter, back-packing through Vietnam. She writes us postcards from that sorry country. After more than ten years of attention from more than half-a-million US combat troops and God knows how many bombs, it is still ravaged by poverty, disease and power politics. In the 1960s, the Malaysians, together with the British and their allies, also made a huge investment of resources and effort, and sacrificed lives, to keep the Indonesians out. But in the whole Borneo campaign there were only five bombs that I knew of, all planted in Singapore by Indonesians and their sympathisers: in the lift shaft of a downtown bank, in a public toilet near Bugis Street, on the Causeway attacking the water pipeline, in the aircraft washing bay at Changi and another on the Shackleton dispersal opposite 215 Squadron. Nine ounces of TNT – made a hell of a bang.

There were no air-strikes in Borneo. In any event, targets would have been difficult to find and hit in the 300-foot trees, but the battle was always for hearts and minds. By not strafing the villages in Kalimantan we lost no friends and made no new enemies. Now, Malaysia is one of the 'Tiger Economies' of Asia.

Apart from the street plan, Singapore is almost unrecognisable from the smelly, disordered but charming colonial city of the 1960s. For the majority of the people that we talk to, it's all the better for it. They have decent housing, a world-famous mass transport system (air-conditioned to boot), and it seems almost no one is without a mobile phone. There's no place here for the sentimental reminiscences of an old airdrop pilot. But we do find an area designated for outdoor eating stalls, where the seafood's just as good, as is the Tiger beer. It's not entirely unexpected to find Bugis Street sanitised – but air-conditioned? A world's first evidently. Sadly, there is not a *kaitai* in sight.

Temple Hill Officers' Mess, now a Malaysian Army HQ and out-of-bounds, is just visible on top of its hill, with the *bashas* alongside. Metal gates and a determined guard prevent us getting any closer. On the other side of the road is a Singapore Air Force museum. There are no Borneo

Campaign exhibits and the young Malay attendant is another who hasn't heard of *Confrontasi*. It seems the conflict has been air-brushed from this particular record. Up on its hill we find the Changi Hospital buildings, weeds growing through the cracked concrete. It is inhabited only by dogs and is apparently earmarked for development. Before our flight home, we find time to walk through Changi Village – very much changed, almost engulfed by the massiveness of Changi International Airport and now a small corner of the global village.

Rumbling down the tarmac, now stretching almost as far as Bedok Corner, the jumbo jet rolls right over the spot where the buildings and aircraft of 215 Squadron stood – and those of the New Zealanders, alongside the Shackletons, and the Survival School. On the climb away, we look down on Changi Gaol, a dark symbol of former conflict in Singapore. I'm glad to have come back to Borneo and Malaysia to see peace at work, where once there was *Confrontasi*.

CHAPTER FOURTEEN

Perspective

By the second half of 1944 the Japanese had been in occupation of much of South East Asia, and the whole of Borneo, for the best part of three years. Allied forces were beginning to counter-attack deep into the Japanese 'Great Co-prosperity Regime', from Burma in the west and New Guinea in the east. Mostly, this counter-attack was heavily armoured, with fleets of ships and aircraft, and with millions of tons of ordnance hurled onto beaches and into jungle, softening up Japanese defences for the brave and bloody assaults of the infantry. Borneo however, was off the main line of these thrusts and a less direct approach was taken.

One morning in late 1944, almost eighteen years to the day before the first mission of 215 Squadron to those mountains, a four-engined American Liberator bomber penetrated for the first but not the last time, the isolation of the natives living at Bario up on the great Plain of Bah. These were the Kelabits, a tribe that had over centuries developed, by using irrigation, a rice-culture unique in the whole of Borneo. At 4,000 feet, encircled by mountains up to 8,000 feet, the Kelabit civilisation was almost untouched by British, Dutch or Japanese doctrine. Their trade in rice and salt had been disrupted and then commandeered by the Japanese, so the Allies judged they would be welcome at their longhouses and chose their plain as a strategic base for mounting a guerrilla campaign against the Japanese from within.

Hence the arrival of a great silver bird roaring in from over the white Tamabo cliffs, and the manifestation of four gods floating down from the sky through the morning mist. These gods were three Australians and their leader, an Englishman – the renowned Tom Harrisson.

Over the next months, until the summer of 1945, these Special Operations personnel mobilised the native tribes against the Japanese occupying forces. A total of 100,000 tribesmen joined up within the first ten weeks.

The Japanese were concentrated along the coasts and made their main naval and air base on Labuan island. In May and June 1945 amphibious forces, mainly Australians reinforced with 1,000 Americans, launched assaults on Borneo, through the port of Tarakan, some 150 miles east of Bario.

On 10 June, Allied troops landed at Labuan. The War Cemetery and Memorial there is still tended by the Commonwealth War Graves Commission. Here lie the remains of 3,908 soldiers who died either in captivity or in action in the liberation, most being Australian but with others from New Zealand and India, as well as the local combatants. They were carried to the cemetery from all over Borneo and many are known 'only unto God'.

In early 1945, hundreds died when the Japanese, anticipating an Allied landing on the Borneo east coast, force-marched prisoners from Sandakan, on the infamous Ranau Death March. Those that were left at Sandakan died of malnutrition and disease, or were killed by their captors.

At first the Allies met fierce opposition and suffered heavy casualties, but Japanese strength was sapped when the natives denied them food and support. The Japanese were forced to fall back, following the rivers up to the highlands.

The guerrillas, marshalled by Tom Harrisson and his colleagues, tracked the fleeing Japanese, and harried them at every turn. With shotguns, spears, *parangs* and poisoned blowpipe darts they took their revenge. The Ibans or Sea Dyaks, lowland tribes with longhouses by the rivers, were more exposed to deprivations by the Japanese. They, the original piratical 'wild men of Borneo', therefore had particular reason to even the score, and many a new head was added to the collection in the rafters of their ancestral smoke-vaults, reportedly for a bounty of 'ten bob a knob'. The swarming *Semut* (Ants), a force 6,000-strong, inflicted more than 1,700 casualties on the Japanese.

After the nuclear attack on the Japanese homeland in August and the end of the war in the Far East, Harrisson was obliged drastically to revise these tactics, for the Japanese were at a stroke 'friends'. There now came an urgent need to resolve the colonial tensions on Borneo island. The Japanese Empire had gone, although remnants of the occupying forces on Borneo continued to hold out for another two years from the caves in the uplands. The British had been absent only temporarily and, together with their Australian allies, were the liberators. Their colonial rule had been regarded with some affection. In Sarawak there had been two centuries of the Rajah Brooke Dynasty. Although set up by a private adventurer profiting from tribal wars, it was generally seen to have brought great benefit in the way of trade and benevolent law. The British masters were tolerant of native animistic beliefs and spirit-worship, respecting and encouraging local custom and culture. But the Dutch, so unceremoniously kicked out by the Japanese at the beginning of hostilities, wanted to reclaim their colonial possessions in Indonesia, and there was trouble.

An Indonesian Independence Movement existed before the war, and it suited the Japanese to encourage this desire for autonomy. After August 1945, tens of thousands of Japanese troops in the Netherlands East Indies were remote from and unprotected by the homeland. In areas where Indonesian nationalism was strong, they surrendered themselves and their arms to the Nationalist forces. Empowered by this sudden and unexpected turn of events and supported by his militant 'Black Hats' freedom fighters, the Nationalist leader Dr Sukarno proclaimed the Republic of Indonesia on 17 August 1945.

Two days earlier, the American Supremo, General MacArthur, had handed over Allied power in South East Asia to Admiral Mountbatten, and the liberation of PoWs and the establishment of law and order in Indonesia were now the responsibility of the British and their allies. HMS *Cumberland* and its cruiser squadron, on the point of setting sail for home, received orders to sail instead for Batavia (later Djakarta), the Indonesian capital on the island of Java.

It collected *en route* three divisions of the 15th Indian Army Corps and one division of the piping and kilted Cameron and Seaforth Highlanders. Owing to lack of space on the ships, many of these troops were forced to make an appalling six-day voyage from Port Swettenham in Malaya in landing-craft.

The formal capitulation of the Japanese was accepted on HMS *Cumberland* moored off Batavia on 15 September. So began the British and Allied occupation of Indonesia – set to last until the end of November 1946.

Expecting to be at home with their wives and families in India and Inverness, the Allied troops found themselves pitched instead, into an extraordinarily confused post-war maelstrom. The first task was to find and liberate the inmates of the Japanese internment camps. The Australians who had been fighting in Borneo at the war's end liberated the internees there, relieved in January 1946 by the British who continued to mop up the Japanese die-hards in the jungle. But there were some 2,000 British and Allied PoWs incarcerated in harsh tropic jungles on the island of Sumatra (1,000 miles long) and of Java (600 miles). These camps took some finding. The natives were generally not hostile towards the inmates as the British were well thought of and had been ever since the liberal reforms of Sir Stamford Raffles during his occupation of Java in the

Napoleonic Wars. By the end of September all these internees had been set free.

The 100,000 Dutch and Eurasian prisoners in Sumatra and Java were another matter. Thousands of Indonesian nationalists, many with Japanese arms as well as *kris* (murderous sinuous-bladed daggers) and shotguns, were determined to slaughter as many as possible of these prisoners. They were seen as either hated ex-colonial masters or Japanese collaborators – or both. Many Dutch internees liberated themselves from the camps, went back to their pre-war businesses and raised the Dutch flag – inviting immediate hostility from the Indonesians. Batavia itself became a battle-zone, with scores of kidnaps and murders, and the Dutch fought back, tooth and nail.

The Indonesian dictatorship saw the need for negotiation but lacked control. There was mayhem – trains and convoys were ambushed, prison camps stormed, assassinations and atrocities committed. The Japanese, so recently the fiercest of enemies, were rearmed under British orders, to guard the camps against attack from the Indonesians, alongside British troops.

At Soerabaya in East Java on 8 October 1945, Dutch prisoners left the camp against orders and raised their flag in the town. They were slaughtered by a mob. There was intense fighting for a month, with 400 Allied and 6,000 Indonesian casualties, before the liberation of the 10,000 internees. At Amberawa in Central Java there were another 10,000, and in the action to liberate these, ninety-five Indonesian mortar shells fell on the camp in just one day.

Such actions inspired Nationalist support among the 56,000,000 Indonesian peasants and coolies in Java and Sumatra, crying '*Merdeka!*' from Dutch rule. Indonesia was in a virtual state of war and many of its forces were ferocious. Those trained by the Japanese during the occupation had adopted Japanese methods, including the *Samurai* sword. Others had rejected everything Japanese and had incarcerated thousands in their own prison camps.

Religious and cultural tension added to the fury. In Acjeh and Bantam there was Muslim fanaticism, which had been at odds with colonialism and Buddhism by turn for centuries. But in Christian Ambon there was deep pro-Dutch feeling – on this Moluccan island the massacre of British traders in 1623 was still a proud folk memory. A Javanese, Tan Malacca, who had spent twenty-five years in Tashkent exiled by the Dutch, returned with Russian revolutionary zeal. In addition, the Chinese diaspora began an orgy of retribution, with 1,500 men, women and children massacred in one incident on the island of Sunda.

In the crossfire, the British were required not only to free PoWs, but also to restore order and prevent civil war. The considerable military struggle involved over 90,000 British and Indian troops, not forgetting the Japanese, now fighting alongside the British at the battle of Semarang. There was also a political conundrum. At one stage the Dutch Commander-in-Chief attempted a disastrous coup, unsupported by the British who were more in tune with the aims of the Nationalists, who seemed to embody the will of the people.

Dr Achmed Sukarno had returned from exile and uncorked the chauvinist fervour of three centuries. He was a charismatic leader who drew crowds of 60,000 a time to hear him speak. The British put their trust in the more moderate Indonesian interim Prime Minister, Sjahrir, and steered a path through the various political trap-falls.

The role of the RAF in all this turmoil was crucial. From the main base of Kemajoran on Java flew Thunderbolt and Spitfire fighters, Mosquito bombers, and Austers for air observation. From a 1,600-yard bitumized-hessian runway, in the daily one-and-a-half inches of pouring rain, they operated alongside Dutch Liberator bombers and Catalina amphibians. There were 110 aircraft in all and they churned the airfield into a mud-bath. The RAF Regiment defended the base and bore the brunt of the looting and sniping.

31 Transport Squadron supported the military action. With their sturdy and reliable Dakotas they flew an average of twenty-eight sorties a day – 11,000 in the course of the campaign – carrying nearly 130,000 passengers and 26,000 tons of freight. They ran the blockade of Bandoeng, a vital road and rail junction in central Java, for many weeks and ensured the survival of PoWs and troops besieged in the town.

This squadron and these aircraft had seen distinguished service in Burma, both in the revolutionary and spectacularly successful close air support of the Allied armies and in flying over the infamous 'Hump'. This extraordinary strategic transport exercise, airlifting men, fuel and armaments over the Himalayas from Assam in India to Chungking and Kunming in China, began in 1942 when the Japanese cut the Burma Road through Siam. RAF aircraft reinforced the US Army Air Force in running a shuttle service, up to twelve hours each way in bad monsoon weather over mountains up to 17,000 feet. The air-supply lessons learnt in Burma were brought to the Netherlands East Indies campaign.

The RAF lost forty-two of its personnel in Java and Sumatra, and South East Asia Command (SEAC) lost over 350 killed or missing with a further 1,000 injured. But by the time the cruiser HMS *Cumberland* finally set sail for home, the campaign could be judged a qualified success. Full civil war was avoided, Indonesia had a functioning infrastructure and in the whole of the conflict, not one bridge had been blown or power station or factory destroyed.

But from May 1946, when their forces started to withdraw and hand over to the Dutch, there was much bitterness against the British who were seen as having betrayed the natives to their hated colonial masters. Power in Indonesia was divided between the Nationalists and the Dutch, but only until 1949 when, with United States political backing, the colonialists were sent packing.

In New Guinea, however, the conflict and tension continued until the early 1960s. In 1962, when 41 Squadron RNZAF delivered their Bristol Freighters from Auckland to Singapore via Mokmer in West New Guinea, they found Dutch Air Force pilots stationed there with their Hunters, still fighting the Indonesians. The pilots reckoned they would be winning – if the USA hadn't pulled the rug from under them.

In all this were sown seeds of Confrontation.

Seeds were also sown in another titanic struggle against nationalism – the Malayan Emergency, a conflict that lasted twelve years.

In 1948 Malaya was a rich British colony, producing most of the world's rubber and tin. Of the population of nearly five million, half were Malays, with two million Chinese and the rest of Indian origin. The Chinese were the traders and businessmen, whose success was resented by the Malay majority. The Chinese were fiercely loyal to China where the exploits of Mao Tse Tung led to an upsurge of Communist sympathy in their ranks. The Malayan Communist Party, including their leader Chin Peng, was on the Allied side in the Second World War providing 4,000 guerrillas and 6,000 ancillary personnel in the fight against the Japanese occupiers. By the end of 1945 this force, the Malayan Peoples' Anti-Japanese Army, was 6,000 strong.

After the war the leaders of this movement, with support from China, set out to overthrow the British colonial government by guerrilla warfare. They believed that having thrown out the Japanese in three years, a maximum of six would be needed to defeat the British. In 1948 the sabotage and killings began and on 16 June the new Federation of Malaya invoked emergency powers.

The Malay peninsula is 400 miles north to south and at its maximum, 200 miles east to west. A spinal chain of mountains rises to 7,000 feet. Four-fifths of the terrain was primary jungle with trees rising to 150 feet. Elsewhere were rubber and coconut plantations, rice fields, tin mines, native villages and a few small towns.

As in Borneo, flying conditions were plainly perilous, with monsoon winds and low cloud, tropical storms, torrential rain and severe turbulence. Landing grounds were few, and far apart, and navigation and radio aids basic. The aircraft and aircrews of the RAF and its allies were again vital to success in three areas: strike, reconnaissance and support.

Strike tactics were at their most effective against jungle camps. Carpet-bombing of jungle without such a target was a waste of ordnance. But against identified targets, bombs, rockets and cannon could be used to devastating effect. Reconnaissance on the ground was mostly carried out by the SAS and Special Branch, assisted in the air by the courageous pilots of the Army Air Corps, flying their tiny single-engined Austers across limitless jungle in appalling weather with no diversion or crash-landing options. As in the Dutch East Indies, the workhorse of supply was the Dakota, of which there were four RAF squadrons. They were tasked with trooping (the roads were impassable in remote areas) and leaflet dropping, fifty million being dropped in the campaign. They were assisted from 1956 by a squadron of Single Pioneers making 1,000 difficult landings a year.

Paratroop dropping was limited – a hazardous business in the 200-feet trees, despite experiments with knotted ropes and abseils. It was abandoned altogether when the helicopters arrived. The first of these was a Casevac flight formed in April 1950 at Changi Hospital with three Dragonflies, which flew at just 70 knots over a range of no more than 225 miles. They were upgraded to Sycamores in 1954. Casualty evacuation possibilities were hugely enhanced with the helicopters and contributed massively to troop morale and effectiveness.

The main task of the Dakotas was supply-dropping. Loaded by the RASC with 200-lb SEAC packs, the aircraft delivered rations, clothing, ammunition and medical supplies by parachute to the army patrols in the field.

The Patrol Commander selected the DZ, often just a ten-yard hole in the jungle. He would radio an estimated map reference – at times the patrol itself was unsure of its location – and lay out cloth panels or launch smoke grenades. On good days, radio contact could be made with the dropping aircraft. The aircrews were always pleased to have voice confirmation of the success of the drop. If the packs were lost, 50 feet off-target into the 200-feet trees or the ubiquitous swamp, then the drop would have to be repeated. The parachutes were expensive and their supply limited. Less than half were recovered, of which half again were re-usable. Some 18,000 a year were required at a price, then, of £32 each.

The Dakotas were reinforced in early 1951 by Valettas, and in 1955 by RNZAF Bristol Freighters. The aircrews always operated at 300 feet or below, where it was hottest, and lost up to 3 lb body-weight per man per sortie. In March 1955, 218 supply-dropping sorties were flown delivering 808,000 lb, from just seventeen useable airfields. Payloads became more varied: assault boats, marine engines, water pumps, tractors, earth-moving equipment, furniture and livestock (including cats). Overall, not much more than 1 per cent of supplies dropped were lost.

Such close and frequent support meant the patrols could penetrate deeper into the jungle, operating for months rather than the previous maximum of four days. This in turn meant that the enemy was no longer able to operate unmolested just 5 to 10 miles inside the jungle fringe. They were driven away from the villages and their food supplies, tracked, attacked and eliminated.

The parallels with the Borneo Confrontation supply-dropping campaign are vivid, but we had bigger aircraft and better navaids: they had Dakotas and Valettas – and casualties. The casualty rate in the supply-dropping crews in the Malayan Emergency was four times that of the infantry they were supporting.

In 1951 the Malayan Communist Party (MCP) changed its name to the Malay Races Liberation Army (MRLA), following recognition of the Communist governments of Mao Tse Tung in China by the British, and of Ho Chi Minh in North Vietnam by the Russians. The Communists were attempting by this name change, to win the Malayans over to their cause. But the Security Forces were winning the hearts and minds campaign, by a mixture of force (concentration of the population in secure areas) and incentive (offering fabulous rewards for defection and elimination of guerrillas). By mid-1954 some 7,500 terrorists had been eliminated, and an estimated 3,500 remained in the jungle.

In 1955 the first federal elections were held in Malaya, further reducing the appeal of the Communists, but in 1956 as many as 2,500 terrorists were still resisting. In 1956 and 1957 the air-transports carried a total of supplies nearly three times that of the previous two years.

The last withdrawal of troops from operational areas came in 1960 and emergency regulations were lifted at the end of July. Some 7,000 communist guerrillas had been killed and 4,000 surrendered or were captured, but Chin Peng escaped to Thailand with his remaining entourage and the MRLA never surrendered.

In the whole campaign some 2,000 Malayan civilians were killed, together with 1,000 of their police and 500 British and Allied combatants – Malays, Gurkhas, Australians, New Zealanders, Fijians and East Africans. The courage, dedication and sacrifice of these fighters won the day, supported by intelligence and internment on the ground and strike and supply from the air. The final ace was the granting of independence in 1957 to Prime Minister Tunku Abdul Rahman and the peoples of the Federation of Malaya.

The Communists and Nationalists in Indonesia watched the Malayan struggle for inspiration and example in throwing off the colonial yoke. When in 1962 the British were still in Malaya – and Singapore and Borneo – President Sukarno's determination was reinforced, to see them off through *Confrontasi*.

The extent of military resource available to Sukarno was immense. In 1963 the Indonesian Army numbered 330,000 men in 134 battalions, plus 3,000 Commandos. Of these, 6,000 were within 20 miles of the Borneo frontier. This grew to 13,000 in early 1965. The overwhelming air power was never used, for fear of political uproar and full-scale war. The Indonesian Navy numbered 25,000, including 9,000 marines, equipped with one cruiser, fourteen destroyers and frigates, twelve submarines and twenty-one minesweepers – all Russian-built. They also had fifteen British-built Gannet naval aircraft. Again, these forces seldom came out of their main base at Surabaya, kept there as much by the British Far East Fleet as by politics. The British Naval Commander made his main objective clear: '... putting the fear of God into Indonesians who take to the water.'

From mid-way through 1964, British troops and their allies started to make offensive incursions into Indonesian Borneo. These top-secret operations, code-named 'Claret', were given overall clearance by London, with individual raids authorised by the Director of Operations, General Walker, himself. Tried and tested troops were to be used – and only for hot pursuit and deniable offensive patrols – to seek out Indonesian bases and training camps. Initially, the penetration limit was 3,000 yards, increased to 10,000 in January 1965 as incursions by Indonesian regular troops increased. These operations were never made public, not even by the Indonesians, as Sukarno could not afford to lose face with his own people.

Close air support could not be given to Claret operations except in an extreme emergency but, very late in the campaign, one of the Argosy crews was detailed to fly at least one mission across the border into Indonesia, at night. Its classification was such that even the CO of 215 Squadron was unaware of the plan. Two SOE agents (code names George and Charlie) made a direct approach to the Flight Commanders and a secret briefing was given at Supreme HQ at Collyer Quay. The Flight Commanders flew on the night practices, but as senior officers, were not permitted to fly on the missions. The operating procedure was that the troops on the ground would point flashlights into the sky at 45 degrees, pinpointing the DZ for the crew. They were not told what and to whom they were dropping, but they knew it was over the border. One recorded mission, from Changi on 13 September, lasted a total of thirteen hours, including a night sortie of more than six hours from Labuan – deep into Indonesia. The Argosy landed back at Changi after dawn the following day. The captain of this clandestine crew, Dickie Miller (Art Smith was the navigator and Ginger Lewis the co-pilot) received the Queen's Commendation.

Any number of casualties is too many, but taking into account the confrontational nature of the campaign, those sustained in Borneo were mercifully light. British and Commonwealth troops lost 114 in action and 181 were wounded. There were thirty-six Malaysian civilians killed, fifty-three wounded and four captured. Of the Indonesians, 590 died, 220 were injured and 771 were captured. A total of 439 Gallantry Awards were made to the British and their allies, headed by the Victoria Cross to Gurkha Lance Corporal Rambahadur Limbu, with 58 DSCs, MCs and DFCs, 280 Mentions in Dispatches and Queen's Commendations – and Boss Leary's AFC.

There was controversy over the award of the General Service Medal (GSM) for the campaign. Originally the intention was to award the Borneo clasp (there was already a Brunei clasp for the 1962 action) for service in the operational area or one operational sortie into it. This was later changed to thirty days' operational service or one operational sortie, which led to some recipients of the clasp being asked to return it. But the qualification was later changed to just thirty days' operational service and all was well.

That in the whole of the Borneo campaign there were no fatalities among the supply-dropping transports was extraordinary. According to the official records, the planners had expected losses of at least 5 per cent. The border area between the Indonesian and Malaysian parts of Borneo was, and still is, one of the most inaccessible areas of mountainous jungle anywhere in the world. The safety record clearly owed much to the improvements in navaids, skilled airmanship – and luck.

The British and their allies were at times outnumbered by ten to one, and in 1963 were attempting to dominate the jungle with just six Infantry battalions (one soldier for every 400 yards of frontier) supported by Iban and Land Dyak cross-border scouts. They were triumphant because of the ability of the SAS, Gurkhas and Parachute Regiment to be the eyes, ears and early warning for the main force, right along the 1,000-mile border. They could only be there because of air resupply by the helicopters, Pioneers and the airdrops. Army records show that the airdrop campaign compared very favourably with Burma, north-west Europe in the Second World War, the Berlin Airlift and Korea. Against all the odds, less than one in ten of the containers dropped was lost, and despite an increasingly critical shortage of 'chutes, an army was kept supplied in the field for the complete campaign.

Confrontation ended in August 1966, a peace treaty being signed three months after President Suharto succeeded President Sukarno. It took a year or two to withdraw the British and allied troops from the jungle, and the Beverleys, Hastings, Pioneers, Bristol Freighters and Argosies continued their air support. The Argosy Kuching detachment was withdrawn in August 1966, but October of that year was the busiest month for 215 Squadron to date, with 785 flying hours.

In 1968, the last of the ground troops were withdrawn from Borneo and the country left intact to its people. Many military surplus goods came on the market, including corrugated metal sheeting rescued from the jungle, beer barrels, and 7,000 sheets of PSP at M$2.05 a piece. The same year, 215 Squadron was disbanded, just five years after its triumphant rebirth. Three of its Argosies were flown back to Benson and seven to Cyprus. Number XP446, the aircraft that so nearly plunged to oblivion in the dinghy-hatch incident over the South China Sea, actually crashed ten years later – while supplying a mysterious missile-firing range, in another jungle, deep in the Congo.

When the last trooping flight had landed at Brize Norton, when Labuan had been handed over to the RMAF, and Indonesia was an ally once more, the Rt. Hon. Denis Healey, now Secretary of State for Defence in Harold Wilson's government, rose to his feet in the Commons to declare:

When the House thinks of the tragedy that could have fallen on a whole corner of a continent if we had not been able to hold the situation and bring it to a successful termination, it will appreciate that in the history books it will be recorded as one of the most efficient uses of military force in the history of the world.

The Borneo Confrontation was Britain's last campaign in Asia.

Appendix

215 Squadron Personnel at Changi

Squadron Commander: Wg Cdr A. Talbot-Williams MA

Engineering Officer: Flt Lt David Birch

Squadron Adjutant: WO Dick Shepherd

Captain:	*Co-pilot:*	*Navigator:*
Flight Commanders:		
Sqn Ldr P. G. Hill-Turner	Flt Lt I. G. Mackie	Flt Lt T. R. Norcross
Sqn Ldr J. M. Leary (AFC Jan '65)	Fg Off R. M. Annett	Flt Lt R. M. Wilkins (Nav Ldr)
Flt Lt G. Garforth (transferred to Wing)	Flt Lt M. R. Smith	Flt Lt E. W. Harrison DFC
Flt Lt J. S. Horrocks	Flt Lt G. D. Taylor (to capt)	Flt Lt J. M. Hare (to Sqn Ldr & Flt Cdr)
Flt Lt R. T. D. Scott	Fg Off D. Lovett	Flt Lt P. H. Verdon
Flt Lt D. Fairbairn	Flt Lt K. McAllen (to capt)	Fg Off G. R. Walker
Flt Lt D. G. Allen	Fg Off P. J. Gorman	Fg Off A. C. Ewer
Flt Lt A. McF. Adams	Fg Off W. M. N. Cross	Fg Off D. J. Parkinson
Flt Lt B. A. Stevens	Fg Off J. B. Davies	Flt Lt D. S. Gates
Flt Lt J. B. Black	Fg Off B. P. Nicolle	Fg Off T. J. Sneddon
Flt Lt R. A. Miller (Queen's Commendation '65)	Fg Off R. R. Lewis	Fg Off J. A. Smith
Flt Lt H. G. Mitchell	Fg Off P. A. Fish	Fg Off R. M. Cooper
Flt Lt J. Horsfall	Fg Off E. Deacon	Flt Lt H. G. Westell
Flt Lt R. Tunnicliffe	Flt Lt A. C. Baker	Flt Lt D. Clements
Fg Off D. G. Thompson	Fg Off D. Marshall	Fg Off K. H. Graham

Flight Engineers:	**Air Quartermasters:**
Flt Lt Dennis Hollingsworth (Engineer Leader)	Master AQM 'Paddy' Kane
Master Eng ('Mister') Howarth (25 years' service tankard '64)	Flt Sgt 'Paddy' O'Loughlin
Master Eng 'Chalky' White	Flt Sgt Colin Bateman
Master Eng Bruce Meteer (25 years' service tankard '64)	Flt Sgt J. R. 'Pete' Jillings
Master Eng 'Jock' Stewart	Flt Sgt Ken Watson
Master Eng 'Smudge' Smith	Flt Sgt Jack Winyard
Flt Sgt Jim Coates	Sgt Geoff Longmuir
Flt Sgt 'Tug' Wilson	Sgt Bob Hodges
Sgt Eric Goodall	Sgt 'Taff' Howell
Sgt R. 'Eddy' Godwin	Sgt John Donnelly
Sgt Pete Webb	Sgt Rex Giles
Sgt Ken Parkinson	Sgt Pat Halliday
Sgt Don Farrow	Sgt Brian Bascoby
Sgt John Meacher	Sgt Jimmy Harris
	Sgt Duncan Macintosh

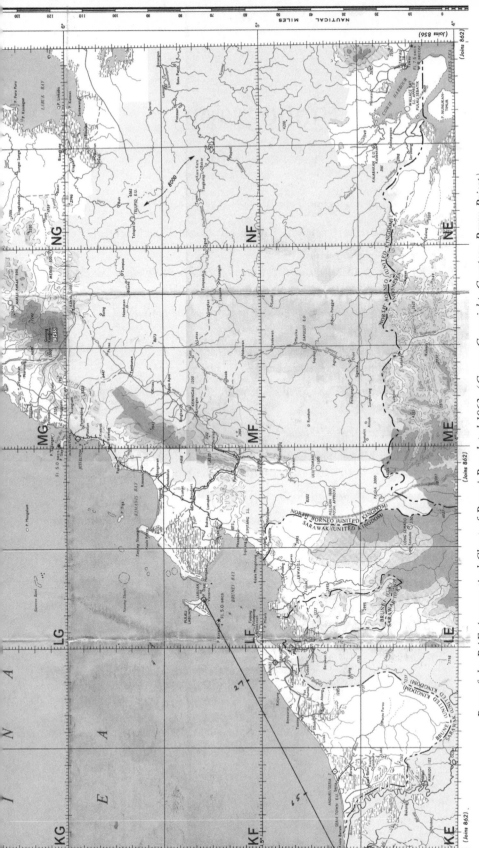

Part of the RAF Aeronautical Chart of Brunei Bay dated 1963. (Crown Copyright, Courtesy Barry Priest)

Bibliography

Air Clues magazine (various), Royal Air Force Directorate of Flight Safety, HMSO.

Dickens, Peter, *SAS: The Jungle Frontier – 22 SAS Regiment in the Borneo Campaign 1963–1966*, Arms & Armour Press (1983).

Geraghty, Tony, *Who Dares Wins: The Story of the SAS 1950 to the Gulf War*, Warner Books.

Guide to Singapore and Spotlight on Malaysia, 16th edn, Papineau Advertising, Singapore (December 1962).

Harclerode, Peter, *PARA: Fifty Years of the Parachute Regiment,* Arms & Armour Press (1992).

Harrisson, Tom, *World Within: A Borneo Story*, Cresset Press (1959).

Lee, Air Chief Marshal Sir David, *Eastward: – A History of the Royal Air Force in the Far East 1945–1972*, HMSO (1984).

Nelles Guide to Malaysia (1995).

Probert, Squadron Leader H. A., *The History of Changi*, RAF Education Flight, Changi (1965).

RAF Forms 540, RAF Air Historical Branch, Bentley Priory.

Van der Post, Laurens and Murray, John, *The Admiral's Baby*, William Morrow & Co. (1997).

Index